Growing a Soul
on the Planet Earth

Ingrid
birthday, family and love —
your father

Growing a Soul on the Planet Earth

The Fourth Way & Esoteric Christianity, Techniques & Practices

Ron and Claire Levitan

Arete Communications
Fairfax, California

Copyright © 2018 by Ron and Claire Levitan.

Cover design by WordPlay Consulting, Santa Rosa, California
korman@wp-consulting.com

Library of Congress Control Number:		2018903597
ISBN:	Softcover	978-1-5434-7991-1
	eBook	978-1-5434-7990-4

All rights reserved. No part of this book may be reproduced or transmitted in any form or by any means, electronic or mechanical, including photocopying, recording, or by any information storage and retrieval system, without permission in writing from the copyright owner.

Arete Communications
773 Center Boulevard, #58
Fairfax, California 94978-0058
Email: Arete@TheGurdjieffLegacyFoundation.org
Website: www.gurdjiefflegacy.org

To order additional copies of this book, contact:
Xlibris
1-888-795-4274
www.Xlibris.com
Orders@Xlibris.com
732418

CONTENTS

INTRODUCTION xi

    The Question of the Soul xiv
    The Purpose of This Book xv

CHAPTER ONE
THE FOURTH WAY 1

    As We Are—As We May Be 3
    Self-Remembering: The Esoteric Key 6
    Developing Higher Being-Bodies 8
    The Second Being-Body: The Kesdjan Body 11
    The Third Being-Body: The Mental Body 15
    The Fourth Being-Body: The Soul 15
    The Megalocosmos & Our Role in It 18
    Techniques & Practices: The Megalocosmos within Us ... 21
    Conclusion 22

CHAPTER TWO
ANCIENT EGYPT 24

    Ancient Egyptian Knowledge & Symbology 25
    Man's Relation to the Cosmos 28
    Horus & Set 30
    Growing a Soul 33
    Conclusion 37

CHAPTER THREE
CHRISTIANITY..39

    The Soul in the Gospels of the New Testament.....................41
    Paul—The Thirteenth Apostle 45
        Paul's Life & Writings 46
        Paul's Theory of the Soul 47

CHAPTER FOUR
AUGUSTINE & AQUINAS 53

DEVELOPING THE TRADITIONAL CHRISTIAN
THEORY OF THE SOUL 53

    Augustine of Hippo..54
        His Life & Writings 54
        Augustine's Theory of the Soul..57
    Thomas Aquinas 63
        His Life & Writings 63
        Aquinas's Theory of the Soul...66

CHAPTER FIVE
ESOTERIC CHRISTIANITY & THE FOURTH WAY 71

    The Fourth Way & the Origins of Esoteric Christianity............71
    Esoteric Christianity in the Gnostic Gospels 75
    The Esoteric Teachings of Paul & The Fourth Way 84
    The Gospel of Judas 89
    Conclusion 92

AFTERWORD..95

    How to Create a Soul 96
    Involution or Conscious Evolution?..96

APPENDIX 101

   Zoroastrianism 101
      Zarathustra's Life 102
      Zoroastrianism & the Soul 104
      Zarathustra's One God 105
      Creation through Opposition 105

   John Milton, the Mortalists & the Soul 108
      John Milton 108
      Milton's Views on the Soul 110
      Milton's Materialism 112
      Milton, Immortality & the Resurrection 113
      Milton & the Mortalists 114
      Nott, Saurat & Gurdjieff's Teaching on the Soul 117
      Milton's Esotericism 120

ENDNOTES 131

SELECTED BIBLIOGRAPHY 161

INDEX 169

To our teacher,
William Patrick Patterson,
and to our fellow students
with whom we share this incredible journey
from the unreal into the Real

INTRODUCTION

"DO YOU HAVE A SOUL?"

MOST OF US THINK THE ANSWER IS "YES, I WAS BORN WITH A SOUL." After all, the major religions of the West—Christianity, Islam, and Judaism—all teach that we are born with a soul.[1] We believe our soul gives us the capacity to make choices and, barring accidents and catastrophes, we have control over our lives. And so, our only concern and fear is not to lose our soul.

But *why* do we believe we have a soul? Have we ever really examined the reason for our belief? Or do we simply accept, without question, our parents' religion and what we were taught? Perhaps we believe we have a soul because most people think so and most people must be right. Is it that life would be meaningless if there is nothing after death? Or perhaps we are engaged in spiritual practices that make no real mention of the soul, or we simply accept the doctrines on the soul that accompany these practices as tangential to our spiritual pursuits.

To learn what people today think about the question of the soul, we began asking total strangers, such as store clerks ringing up our purchases, as well as acquaintances and friends. Much to our surprise, strangers and mere acquaintances often engaged the question earnestly, not trying to shake off these apparently crazy people asking such a strange question.

---

[1] In contrast to the major religions of the West, Buddhism has the doctrine of *annata/anatman*, "no soul" or impermanence.

Virtually everyone said they had a soul.[2] In some cases, when the chemistry was right, we asked the reason for their belief. Some said their beliefs were based on ingrained childhood religions, others just assumed they had a soul, and others said they had a soul because they were Christian and would be saved by their belief in Jesus Christ. When asked what their souls were made of, it was clear from the uncomfortable pauses—having just confidently expressed their belief in the soul's existence—that they were now faced with a question they had never considered before. Some were engaged by the question and admitted they did not know, some recovered by saying the soul is immaterial, others related it to the mind in some tentative fashion, and one person said it was "stardust."

The few who said they did not have a soul were proudly atheist and insisted there is nothing beyond human life. Some portrayed themselves as humanists, espousing the position that there is intrinsic value in doing good and helping others. While secularism is a growing movement in this country, we didn't speak to many who defined themselves in this way.[3] Regardless of each person's orientation to the question, no one was actively engaged in exploring the question.

The question was the subject of W. Somerset Maugham's classic *The Razor's Edge*. While Maugham called the book a novel, he did

---

[2] A 2005 Princeton Survey Research / Newsweek poll found that 85 percent of respondents believe they have a soul. More recently, in a 2014 CBS News poll, 66 percent of respondents said they believed in heaven and hell, 11 percent in heaven only, and 17 percent in neither; interestingly, among the 77 percent who believed in heaven, 82 percent believed they were going there themselves. *See* Kathleen Weldon, "Paradise Polled: Americans and the Afterlife," *HuffPost*, www.huffingtonpost.com/kathleen-weldon/paradise-polled-americans_b_7587538.html.

[3] Phil Zuckerman, a professor of sociology who chairs the Secular Studies Program at Pitzer College in California, says surveys suggest that the secular movement is the fastest growing religious orientation in the country, having grown by over 200 percent in the past twenty-five years. According to a 2015 Pew Survey, 36 percent of those born between 1990 and 1996 are religiously unaffiliated. "Altogether, the religiously unaffiliated now account for 23 percent of the adult population, up from 16 percent in 2007." (http://www.pewforum.org/2015/05/12/americas-changing-religious-landscape/).

so because he didn't know what else to call it, but he avowed it was based on fact. The protagonist Larry, an American living in Paris, tries to explain to his fiancée, Isabel, why he does not want to return to Chicago, get a job, and live a traditional married life. Instead, he wants to continue his pursuit into the "lands of the spirit."

"What do you expect to find in them?" she asks.

"The answers to my questions." He gave her a glance that was almost playful, so that except that she knew him so well, she might have thought he was speaking in jest. "I want to make up my mind whether God is or God is not. I want to find out why evil exists. I want to know whether I have an immortal soul or whether when I die it is the end."

Isabel gave a little gasp. It made her uncomfortable to hear Larry say such things, and she was thankful that he spoke so lightly, in the tone of ordinary conversation, that it was possible for her to overcome her embarrassment.

"But Larry," she smiled, "people have been asking those questions for thousands of years. If they could be answered, surely they'd have been answered by now."

Larry chuckled.

"Don't laugh as if I'd said something idiotic," she said sharply.

"On the contrary I think you've said something shrewd. But on the other hand you might say that if men have been asking them for thousands of years it proves they can't help asking them and have to go on asking them. Besides, it's not true that no one has found the answers. There are more answers than questions, and lots of people have found answers that were perfectly satisfactory for them."

Another, more recent, example of someone deeply questioning his belief appeared in the *New York Times Magazine* in December 2016. Bart Campolo, a successful Christian preacher like his father, had a severe bicycle accident, losing whole patches of his memory. When he healed about a month later, "he had a thought about life—or, rather the afterlife. The thought was: There is no life after life." As he said, "After the bike crash I was like, 'A, this is it, and B, you don't know how much of it you've got.'" Apparently assuming he could never grow what he didn't already have—that is, a soul—he abandoned his Christian faith and became a preacher of secular humanism.

How often do *we* squarely face and feel the fact of our own life and our own mortality *in this moment*? Don't we live our lives as if we are immortal? Everyone would, of course, acknowledge that they are going to die—*someday*. But based on the informal survey we conducted, it appears that any fleeting question of the soul remains just that—*fleeting*. Conversely, if there is a deeply held religious belief in the existence of the soul, is the basis for that belief examined?

Growing up, both of us assumed we had a soul and all would turn out well in the end because, after all, we are good people. Claire, raised Catholic, was indoctrinated with the Catholic Church's teachings about the soul. Ron was raised nominally as a Jew, and Jews don't talk much about the soul or the afterlife. But after all, Jews are "The Chosen People," so who's to worry?

The Question of the Soul

We did not come directly to the question of the soul. We came to it through disillusionment with the apparent purposes of human life and our nascent recognition that *I am not what I take myself to be*. For many years, we searched and inconsistently pursued a variety of spiritual teachings and practices, including meditation and self-help/spiritual books, becoming temporarily enamored of certain authors whose books ultimately did nothing for us. We even found some faux teachers. Finally, we discovered the ancient esoteric teaching of The Fourth Way, introduced to the West in 1912 by Georgi Ivanovitch Gurdjieff, one of the greatest spiritual messengers of the last century. We have been extremely fortunate to find a Fourth Way teacher in the direct lineage of Mr. Gurdjieff, and together with other like-minded students, pursue the answers to our questions concerning the soul through the practices of this ancient teaching.

To ask what is a soul and whether or not I have one is to strive to understand what it means to be a human being. To begin at the beginning:

- Was I born with a soul?
- Does every human being actually have one?
- If I have a soul, where did it come from?
- What is it made of?
- Is a soul just dormant within me, waiting for death so it, or "I", can be rewarded or punished for my actions?
- What is the soul's relationship to my body?
- If souls do exist outside the physical body, what actually happens to my soul when I die?

As noted above, for those of us in the Western world, the almost universal assumption underlying answers to these questions is that we are born with a soul and the soul continues in some form after the body dies. Theories diverge somewhat when addressing the fate of the soul after death.

The Purpose of This Book

But what if, as Mr. Gurdjieff teaches, we are *not* born with a soul? What if immortality, the life after death that most of us assume awaits us, is not a birthright? What if, instead, we are born with the substances to grow a soul and must work consciously to transform them in order to develop a soul? This is an integral aspect of Gurdjieff's Fourth Way, a long-hidden, ancient, esoteric teaching of spiritual self-development and transformation. Gurdjieff did not create this teaching. He discovered it in his quest to answer his question, "What is the sense and significance of life on earth and human life in particular?"

What follows is our effort to understand Gurdjieff's answer to that question. In the first chapter, we explore Gurdjieff's teaching of The Fourth Way, the sacred science of Being that he discovered and reformulated for the West in modern times. In the second chapter, we explore the source teaching that Gurdjieff discovered in ancient Egypt, which answered his question and is the foundation of The Fourth Way. This ancient teaching, as Gurdjieff tells us, is also the foundation of esoteric Christianity, that aspect of Christianity that has nearly been lost. In the third and fourth chapters, we examine the orthodox teachings of Christianity on the soul. And in the fifth chapter, we explore the deep connections between The Fourth Way and esoteric Christianity.

The purpose of this book is not simply to provide a history of the teaching on growing a soul. Our wish is that this book will actively engage you, the reader, in the questions raised. Real answers to these questions cannot come from a book but only from active participation in the practices of self-transformation under the guidance of a teacher. The sacred science of The Fourth Way is not based on faith or dogma; instead, each student verifies through his or her own lived experience the truths of the teaching. As we have discovered, and we hope you will see, only Gurdjieff's teaching of The Fourth Way provides the complete knowledge and practical techniques by which we can transform ourselves spiritually, developing Conscience, Consciousness and Being, that is—*growing a soul.*

CHAPTER ONE

THE FOURTH WAY

Man in his history has always believed he had a soul and sought for it. This is the aim of all religions. If in ordinary life I were asked if man has a soul, I would say no, because in general man has not. Before man can have a soul, he must have an "I." Only when he achieves an "I" can he develop a soul. [4]

—G. I. Gurdjieff

CAN WE CONSIDER THE POSSIBILITY THAT WE DO NOT HAVE A SOUL? IF SO, AREN'T WE LIVING OUR LIFE TRYING TO KEEP WHAT, IN FACT, WE DON'T HAVE? Certainly the common belief that we all have a soul has been a social good, but at what cost? Perhaps at the cost of the truth.[5] For if it is true we have

---

[4] Throughout his writings, Gurdjieff uses the term "man" in the generic sense to refer to humankind.

[5] As some recent philosophers have discerned, esoteric teachings are hidden in the works of philosophers, from Plato to Spinoza, whose exoteric writings veil a secret teaching. For example, Leo Strauss, an eminent philosopher who wrote in the mid-twentieth century, stated, "An exoteric book contains then two teachings: a popular teaching of an edifying character, which is in the foreground; and a philosophic teaching concerning the most important subjects, which is indicated only between the lines." Leo Strauss, "Persecution

no soul, then at death, no matter how good or bad our lives, we are, as Gurdjieff says, "fertilizer." Fortunately, *if* we are strong enough to accept that truth as a possibility, there is a greater truth: we can make and grow a soul—for *we are images of God.*

We have no God-given soul yet are images of God, and so each of us has the possibility to make a soul. These two fundamental truths were brought to the West by Georgi Ivanovitch Gurdjieff. Yes, we are images, but *undeveloped* images. Each of us has a seed, a germ, which gives the possibility of developing a soul. Gurdjieff called it "the representative of God in the Essence."

The teaching of how to make a soul was an ancient scientific system that was, as he said, "completely self-supporting and independent of other [spiritual] lines and it has been completely unknown up to the present time." While human beings have the possibility of becoming immortal, of growing a soul, an inner knowledge and sustained and specific practices and perspectives are required to fulfill this potential. The teaching of The Fourth Way provides both a method and "a mathematical and material explanation of the creation, maintenance and purpose of the universe, man's place in that universe, his function and duty." It is a sacred science of Being, of how to develop a soul, to attain immortality. Said Gurdjieff, "Only by understanding the

---

and the Art of Writing," *Social Research*, 8:4 (1941), 488, 503. As Strauss says, "The exoteric presentation of the truth makes use of statements which are considered by the philosopher himself to be statements, not of facts, but of mere possibilities." That is, "he does not strictly speaking, believe in the truth of [the] statement," which is "addressed to morally inferior people, who ought to be frightened by such statements." The concept of the eternal damnation, which necessarily invokes its counterpart, heaven, and of course the existence of a soul, serves this purpose. Leo Strauss, "Strauss on G. E. Lessing," https://archive.org/stream/LeoStraussOnEsotericismExoterisim/Straus-ExotericTeaching_djvu.txt. As Patterson explains, "It makes . . . good crowd control as it focuses people on living as good a life as possible so they are much easier to govern and otherwise manipulate." William Patrick Patterson, "What Are Humans For?" *The Gurdjieff Journal*, Vol. 18, No. 4, 4. A detailed examination of the difference between exoteric and esoteric teachings can be found in chapter five, "Esoteric Christianity and The Fourth Way."

correct sequence of development possible will people cease to ascribe to themselves what, at present, they do not possess, and what, perhaps, they can only acquire after great effort and great labor."

As We Are—As We May Be

We see life "topsy-turvy," as Gurdjieff said. Our fundamental problem is that we all believe and think of ourselves as individuals. This idea is reinforced in a variety of ways. For example, we are called by a certain name, are held responsible for our actions and inactions, are enmeshed in habits, say "I" to everything, and have some bodily sense, all brought together with our unquestioned belief in ourselves as being an indivisible "I" existing throughout past, present and future space and time. We fail to see that we ordinarily function like a machine and that our childhood conditioning creates a self-image, causing us to react and identify with external or internal stimuli just as a machine acts in accordance with its programming.

Moreover, with the advancement of technology, progress is seen as human functioning in greater collaboration with machines. Thus, though unstated, we aspire to become more efficient machines. The indoctrination into technologizing ourselves starts quite young. For example, a television commercial for a smartphone shows several young children sitting around a table in what looks like a kindergarten classroom with a man in a business suit. The children readily agree with him that doing two things at once is preferable to doing just one, as the voiceover reinforces that idea, "It's not complicated, doing two things at once is better, and only AT&T's network lets you talk and surf on your iPhone." The real point is that at a very young age, particularly in recent times, we see individual human progress as being attained by increasing our collaboration with technology, because with it we can "do" more and do it faster, better.

Scientist, inventor and author Ray Kurzweil, who has been described by *Forbes* magazine as "the ultimate thinking machine," makes this point to a more sophisticated audience. He describes a biotechnology revolution leading to science creating "designer babies" and invading the human body with robotic red blood cells, thereby increasing human capacities. He also foresees implanting into our brains nanobots that will shut down the signals received from our senses, replacing them with signals from a virtual reality that will allow for what he calls full immersion into a virtual reality that can be shared with other people. He describes all this as an expansion of human intelligence through direct merger with technology. He predicts that a "singularity" will be achieved in which humans will transcend the limitations of the body and brain so that "future machines will be human, even if they are not biological." As he has recently described, in his vision our brains will be connected to a neocortical annex in the cloud. "For a time, we'll be a hybrid of biological and nonbiological thinking, but, as the cloud keeps doubling, the nonbiological intelligence will predominate." He concludes by saying that "it will be anachronistic, then, to have one body." The ultimate vision is to "change the definition of human. As each of our functions is uploaded or replaced, at some point you stop calling that a human and start calling it an A.I." [6]

Gurdjieff teaches that we need to see ourselves not as the indivisible I that we think we are but as what we actually are—*an assemblage of different "I"s*. Careful observation will verify that one "I" thinks, speaks or acts, followed by another "I" and another and another. Thoughts, feelings and impulses, all based on conditioned memory, are in continual reaction to outer and inner influences, and we name each of these reactions "I". These "I"s emerge from the three centers of which we are composed—the mental center, the emotional center and the instinctive-moving-sexual center. [7] The past is living the present. We have no indivisible "I", and thus no real will. Instead, "everything happens." We are being lived, not living. All this is to be verified, not believed.

---

[6] *The New Yorker* describes two scientific approaches to the quest for immortality: "Those who might be called the Meat Puppets" who "believe that we can retool our biology and remain in our bodies." The second camp, led by Kurzweil, is called the RoboCops, who "believe that we'll eventually merge with mechanical bodies and/or with the cloud." Tad Friend, "The God Pill: Silicon Valley's Quest to Live Forever," *The New Yorker*, April 3, 2017, 65.

[7] At times the reference will be to one aspect of this tripartite center based on the source of the manifestation of the I, instinctive, moving or sexual.

Can you reconstruct moments in your life when you bounced from "I" to "I" in reaction to external events and internal reactions to those events? Suppose you are in a hurry, late for an appointment, driving down the road when you see that the light ahead is green and has been for a while. An apprehension arises that you may not make it through before the light turns red. You accelerate as the light turns yellow, but the car immediately ahead of you stops for the yellow light. You have to slam on the brakes. You react to the driver in the other car with anger and frustration, perhaps even uttering a curse. Then an old song comes on the radio bringing back memories from a high school romance. Suddenly the red-light frustration evaporates as you are transported back in time. Then your cell phone rings; your spouse is calling to tell you that you forgot your gym bag . . . and so your day goes. We mostly fail to see the significance of this by writing off our reactions as a change in mood, when in reality there is a deep pattern of emotional, physical and mental responses associated with each "I" that reacts.

Living this passive life, controlled first by one "I" then another, we nevertheless fulfill the role that nature requires of us by living in a state of waking sleep. Our mechanical purpose on earth is to do exactly what we are doing right now. Simply by functioning—breathing, moving, associating, thinking—we mechanically receive, process and transmit energies. There are higher energies that we can work with, but Nature neither needs nor compels us to do so. And at death we cease to be. "If a man is changing every minute, if there is nothing in him that can withstand external influences, it means that there is nothing in him that can withstand death. But if he becomes independent of external influences, if there appears in him something that can live *by itself*, this something may not die. In ordinary circumstances we die every moment. External influences change and we change with them; that is, many of our "I"s die." The "I" that "dies" in one moment will, however, be "born again," will emerge again in response to similar stimuli over and over again. Gurdjieff tells us that it is impossible to talk of any kind of immortality for such a person: "Who is now one, the next moment another, and the next moment a third, has no future of any kind; he is buried and that is all." But we can learn to work and develop beyond the life of the "I-of-the-moment."

Self-Remembering: The Esoteric Key

A leading exponent of the teaching, William Patrick Patterson, who studied under Lord John Pentland, the man Gurdjieff appointed to lead the teaching in America, tells us that Gurdjieff did not have to modify *sensing, remembering,* and *observing* with the word *self,* but he did so for a reason. In his series of introductory talks on Gurdjieff's Fourth Way, entitled "From Selves to Individual Self to The Self," Patterson explains, "The teaching extends from the self that we all take ourselves to be, which is really many selves, to the individual self to The Self." Patterson states that the aim of The Fourth Way is to enable us "to recognize that eternal truth within ourselves, moving up through the various levels that begin with the acceptance that I may not be who I think I am." This recognition can only be achieved through the twin practices of self-remembering and self-observation, which begin with self-sensing. "Gurdjieff stressed the need for the activation of *self-sensing* which is the ground of the practice he calls *self-remembering.* Repeatedly, Gurdjieff spoke of the 'instinctive *sensing* of reality,' of the 'instinctive *sensing* of certain cosmic truths,' and he said that 'sensation cannot be expressed intellectually, because it's organic.'" By self-sensing, we can engage in self-remembering, which enables us to be self-conscious, not in the psychological meaning of the phrase—embarrassed or shy—but true self-consciousness, which is the state when we divide our attention simultaneously between both the subject, the "I", and the object, the "it." This requires redirecting our attention from the formatory mind, the source of our constant mechanical associative thoughts, to the sensation of our body. The fluidity of the term *self-remembering* is exemplified by Patterson's further explanation:

> To have consciousness of self is not only to be aware of oneself mentally (in which case it would only be the mind looking at the mind), but also physically and emotionally; that is, a global awareness inclusive of the facticity of the triadic instinctive-sexual, emotional and intellectual functioning. This demands a certain quality and strength of attention, a direct recognition of the *Immediate,* of what-is, of having an awareness that is global in reference to oneself. Consciousness of self is a state predicated on

self-remembering—a conscious awareness of the body, of being embodied, of being connected with what is happening internally; as well as what is happening externally. [Emphasis in original].

Self-observation can only take place while *self-remembering*. "Once embodied, self-observation has physical support . . . As we become relatively more whole, what is observed and experienced also has greater wholeness." Patterson relates that Gurdjieff once succinctly explained self-remembering by stating that it allows you "to know you are angry when you are angry," meaning to experience the anger, the tensions throughout the body, the facial contortions, the tone of voice, and not identify with the anger. That is, knowing how one is manifesting, outwardly or inwardly, with all three centers—intellectual, emotional, instinctual. Through this practice, "one can observe how all things, from the gross to the subtle, appear and disappear in consciousness. A consciousness cleansed of identification with its content is thus without personal referent. One realizes that the body appears in consciousness and not otherwise." Thus, the "teaching extends from the lowest idea of the self to the very highest."

As Gurdjieff says, "The whole secret is that one cannot work for a future life without working for this one. In working for life a man works for death, or rather, for immortality . . . In studying his own life as he knows it, and the lives of other men, from birth to death, a man is studying all the laws which govern life and death and immortality. If he becomes master of his own life, he may become master of his death."

Gurdjieff uses a metaphor to demonstrate how The Fourth Way differs from other teachings that fail to work with the entirety of the human being:

> There are four ways. Let us compare ordinary man with a three-room apartment. The dining room will represent his organism, his moving center, the place where he eats and attends to the needs of the body maintenance and development. The drawing room represents his feeling center and the bedroom his mental center. But this apartment lacks a bathroom which we will call the I room. In man's ordinary three-room apartment there is disorder. The roof leaks in

the dining room or there is no floor in the drawing room or the window panes are broken. The building itself may be in the slums.

Man has tried three ways to find the soul. First by living only in the dining room, develop the body, give it great tasks and suffering—Fakirism. In the drawing room, Monks—feeling center and psychic experiences. Bedroom—mental center, via knowledge, Yogism.

I am the Representative of The Fourth Way. And I have no *concurrent* rival. For instance, ordinary yogis who do not know these secrets lie for three hours a day to learn how to use air. With my secret shortcuts they could do this in five minutes—in fact, like magic, drink the active elements they need from air out of a glass. [Emphasis in original.]

Developing Higher Being-Bodies

Work with the body begins with efforts of a special character, which can only take place in an authentic esoteric school. Through the practices that are taught, the student comes to see how his or her centers—the thinking, emotional, and moving/instinctive/sexual—function in the moment. In learning to consciously relate to the physical body, the centers are gradually balanced so that no one center is dominant.

Ordinarily, it is rare for us to be aware of our body. Our attention is head-bound, almost always talking to ourselves, the body only coming into view in lust, fear, pain, hunger. While we do possess fully formed higher emotional and intellectual centers, because our lower three centers are not developed and harmonized, no conscious contact can be made with these higher centers. The physical body produces all the necessary functions and allows us to be functionally awake, that is, in the waking state of consciousness. For such a person to speak of the functioning of these higher centers would be like "a blind man speaking of colors, or a deaf man speaking of music." Nevertheless, these higher centers can play a role in the development of higher being-bodies.

Each of us has the potential to develop four bodies. Gurdjieff explains that it is possible for four bodies to exist in the human organism because the physical body has such a complex organization that, under certain conditions, a new independent organism can grow in it, affording a much more convenient and responsive instrument for the activity of consciousness than the physical body. The consciousness manifested in this new body, this second body, is capable of governing it, and it has full power and full control over the physical body. In this second body, under certain conditions, a third body can grow, again having characteristics of its own. The consciousness manifested in this third body has full power and control over the first two bodies, and the third body possesses the possibility of acquiring knowledge inaccessible either to the first or to the second body. In the third body, under certain circumstances, a fourth can grow, which differs as much from the third as the third differs from the second and the second from the first. The consciousness manifested in the fourth body has full control over the first three bodies and itself.

The first body is the physical body, the body we are born with, which is composed of earthly materials. The second body, the *Kesdjan* or astral body, is composed of material of the planetary world. The third is called the mental body, and it is composed of material of the sun. The fourth is the soul, comprising crystallizations received directly from the *Theomertmalogos*, or Word-God. [8] We will explore each of the three higher being-bodies in turn, beginning with the *Kesdjan* body.

---

[8] It is interesting to note that this means Charles Darwin's theory of evolution explaining the appearance of human beings on Earth is incorrect. Under Darwin's theory of natural selection, certain inheritable traits are passed along, eventually forming new species. Yet human beings, composed of material of the planetary world and the sun, could not have evolved from animals composed exclusively of earthly materials. As Ouspensky relates in *Search*, Gurdjieff's system "contradicted the usual modern idea of life having originated so to speak from *below*. In his explanations life came from above." Ouspensky, *In Search of the Miraculous*, 139. This is not to say that plant and animal life did not evolve mechanically. *See* figure one, "The Ray of Creation."

Georgi Ivanovitch Gurdjieff

William Patrick Patterson

The Second Being-Body: The *Kesdjan* Body

A *Kesdjan* body (a combination of two Persian words meaning "vessel of the spirit"), being composed of material of the planetary world and the sun of its solar system, can survive the death of the physical body. The *Kesdjan* body is not immortal in the full sense of the word, because after a certain period of time it also dies. If a *Kesdjan* body is formed, it may be reborn in another planetary body, with the possibility of further perfecting and coating the higher bodies. Therefore, creation of the *Kesdjan* body is the beginning of the development of an immortal soul. Very few of us acquire a *Kesdjan*, or "astral body," as it is also referred to.[9] Says Gurdjieff, "A man without an 'astral body' may even produce the impression of being a very intellectual or even spiritual man, and may deceive not only others but himself." When human beings who never develop a *Kesdjan* body die, their physical body, being composed only of earthly material, returns to the earth. *"It is dust and to dust it returns."*

Gurdjieff tells us, "In order to speak of any kind of future life there must be a certain crystallization, a certain fusion of man's inner qualities, a certain independence of external influences." This fusion, which leads to the creation of a *Kesdjan* body, results from the crystallization that occurs from consciously resisting one's mechanical manifestations. Gurdjieff states, "What may be called the 'astral body' is obtained by means of fusion, that is by means of terribly hard inner work and struggle." Gurdjieff compares the process to that of metallic powders in a vessel, or retort, which are not connected to each other and have no permanent position in the vessel. They may be moved about, from top to bottom or side to side, by any external shaking or tapping of the vessel. This condition, referred to as the "state of mechanical mixture," is unstable, with no possibility of being stabilized.

> But the powders may be fused; the nature of the powders makes this possible. To do this a special kind of fire must be lighted under the retort which, by heating and melting

---

[9] In *Search*, the term "astral body" is used in recounting Gurdjieff's teachings of the four bodies to his students in Russia during the period from 1915 to 1919. *Search*, 40–42.

> the powders, finally fuses them together. Fused in this way the powders will be in the state of a chemical compound. And now they can no longer be separated by those simple methods which separated and made them change places when they were in a state of mechanical mixture. The contents of the retort have become indivisible, "individual." *This is a picture of the formation of the second body.* The fire by means of which fusion is attained is produced by "friction," which in its turn is produced in man by a struggle between "yes" and "no." [Emphasis added].

Conscience plays a vital role in the formation of a second body. To understand its role in the fusion Gurdjieff describes, it is necessary to understand what conscience is. As Gurdjieff says, in ordinary life we take the word *conscience* too simply, as if we have a conscience. But the concept of conscience "in the sphere of the emotions is equivalent to the concept 'consciousness' in the sphere of the intellect. And as we have no consciousness we have no conscience." Thus consciousness is a state in which we know all at once everything we know and in which we can see how little we know and how many contradictions there are in what we know. Conscience "is a state in which a man *feels all at once* everything that he in general feels, or can feel. And as everyone has within him thousands of contradictory feelings which vary from a deeply hidden realization of his own nothingness and fears of all kinds to the most stupid kind of self-conceit, self-confidence, self-satisfaction, and self-praise, to feel all this together would be not only painful but literally unbearable." This description of conscience allows us to grasp the role it plays in the fusion that helps create the *Kesdjan* body.

> Conscience is the fire which alone can fuse all the powders in the glass retort . . . and create the unity which a man lacks in that state in which he begins to study himself.
>
> The concept "conscience" has nothing in common with the concept "morality."

Conscience is the same for all men and conscience is possible only in the absence of "buffers."[10] From the point of view of understanding the different categories of man we may say that there exists the conscience of a man in whom there are no contradictions. This conscience is not suffering; on the contrary it is joy of a totally new character which we are unable to understand. But even a momentary awakening of conscience in a man who has thousands of different "I"s is bound to involve suffering. And if these moments of conscience become longer and if a man does not fear them but on the contrary cooperates with them and tries to keep and prolong them, an element of very subtle joy, a foretaste of the future "clear consciousness" will gradually enter into these moments.

On the other hand, the struggle may occur mechanically or through a wrong foundation, such as a fanatical belief or fear of sin, and thus must be melted down if right crystallization is to occur. Or it may occur through conscious effort, through the practice of *being-Partkdolg-duty*—that is, one may, through conscious labors and intentional sufferings, work to self-remember and divide the attention to self-observe impartially the inner struggle between "yes" and "no." The friction generated is what creates the fire necessary for fusion to occur. In this way, permanent traits begin to form themselves, begin to crystallize within the planetary body. This inner growth is a process that occurs gradually over a long period of time.

---

[10] The term "buffers" is used pointedly. Buffers on railway carriages lessen the shock when carriages strike one another. Without buffers, the shock of one carriage against another would be "very unpleasant and dangerous." We have the same appliances within us for the same purpose. They arise involuntarily due to the many "contradictions of opinions, feelings, sympathies, words and actions. If a man throughout his whole life were to feel all the contradictions that are within him he could not live and act as calmly as he lives and acts now." Buffers allow us to cease to feel the impact from the clash of contradictory views, emotions, and words. Ouspensky, *Search*, 154–55.

The growth of the *Kesdjan* body begins with the proper functioning of the physical body. If ordinary food, air and impressions are taken in *consciously*, the physical body produces the finer substances that are necessary for the growth and feeding of the higher bodies. *Hanbledzoin*, the blood of the *Kesdjan* body, is composed of these finer substances, which are obtained from the transformation of elements of other planets and of the sun of the particular solar system. From this crystallization, finer hydrogens are produced. Over time, with conscious efforts, the whole of the physical body, all its cells, are permeated by emanations of the matter of these hydrogens, and the *Kesdjan* body is formed. This is the transmutation of the "coarse" to the "fine," or the transformation of base metals into gold about which the alchemists spoke. Gurdjieff calls this process the "coating" of the second being-body. What is crystallized cannot be lost and is not subject to decomposition on this planet. By contrast, if a person "has begun to accumulate these substances, but dies before they have crystallized, then simultaneously with the death of the physical body, these substances also disintegrate and become dispersed."

However, when the physical body dies the *Kesdjan* body at whatever stage of its development, being composed of what has been crystallized, rises in accordance with the law of gravity to the sphere where the cosmic substances of which it is made have their concentration. Nevertheless, the *Kesdjan* body cannot remain forever in this sphere, and it may be born again in another physical body. This is what is commonly called "reincarnation," the continuation of life in the *Kesdjan* body or with the help of the *Kesdjan* body. This may happen many times, as a planetary body is needed for the transmutation of the substances necessary to completely coat the *Kesdjan* body. However, Gurdjieff says that the astral body's reincarnation is accidental, unconscious. "If it is not reborn, then, in the course of time, it also dies; it is not immortal but it can live long after the death of the physical body."

Unlike other teachings that use this term and state that all human beings have an astral body, Gurdjieff makes it clear that "only a very few men acquire an 'astral body.'" He tells us "these unfortunate germs of 'higher being-bodies'" are "compelled to languish in all kinds of exterior planetary forms." Gurdjieff teaches us that there is a way to rise above this mechanical languishing. That is, through the practice of *being-Partkdolg-duty*, conscious labors and intentional sufferings, the complete coating of the *Kesdjan* body can occur. Through this process we eventually gain access to the higher emotional center, which, like the higher intellectual center, is formed and fully present in the planetary body. However, these two higher centers are unconnected to the three lower centers. Only by working to perfect the functioning of the human machine through *being-Partkdolg-duty* can these higher centers be accessed. While the *Kesdjan* or astral body and the higher emotional center may sometimes be equated, "they are more correctly understood as different aspects of the next stage of man's evolution. It can be said that the 'astral body' is necessary for the complete and proper functioning of the 'higher emotional center' in unison with the lower. Or it can be said that the 'higher emotional center' is necessary for the work of the 'astral body.'"

The Third Being-Body: The Mental Body[11]

In much the same way, the third or mental body corresponds to the higher intellectual center. But they are not one and the same thing. One requires the other, one cannot exist without the other, and one is the expression of certain sides and functions of the other. If a person has a third body or mental body, it is composed of material of the sun and it can exist after the death of the *Kesdjan* body. Gurdjieff tells us that this body, too, may reincarnate, but unlike the *Kesdjan* body, it is able to choose the physical body it will inhabit. One who develops a third body has the complete knowledge possible, but it can still be lost.

The Fourth Being-Body: The Soul

The fourth body is the soul. "The fourth body," said Gurdjieff, "is composed of material of the *starry world,* that is, of material that does not belong to the solar system, and therefore, if it has crystallized

---

[11] In *Search*, Ouspensky outlines Gurdjieff's description of three higher-being bodies, the astral, the mental, and the soul. *Search*, 40–44. It should be noted that in *All and Everything*, Gurdjieff's magnum opus, he refers to only two higher being-bodies, the *Kesdjan* body and the soul. Gurdjieff, *All and Everything*, 1106.

within the limits of the solar system there is nothing within this system that could destroy it. *This means that a man possessing the fourth body is immortal within the limits of the solar system.*" [Emphasis in original.] The knowledge of this man "is his own knowledge, which cannot be taken away from him; it is the objective and completely *practical* knowledge of *All.*" [Emphasis in original.] When the planetary body dies, the *Kesdjan* body and the fully developed soul separate from the physical body, leaving it on Earth. The two rise up together to the sphere where the cosmic substances that make up the *Kesdjan* body have their place of concentration. They exist there together until the final sacred *Rascooarno* or death occurs to the *Kesdjan* body. The soul then leaves the *Kesdjan* body and becomes an independent individual with its own individual Reason.

However, a soul that is not yet fully developed must continue to perfect its Reason. In that case, it is dependent on the *Kesdjan* body and has to exist in the sphere of the *Kesdjan* body until it has perfected its objective Reason to the requisite degree. The *Kesdjan* body, however, "cannot exist long in this sphere, and at the end of a certain time this second being part must decompose." If that occurs, the crystallizations of which it is composed go in various ways into the sphere of its own primordial arisings. In anticipation of the *Kesdjan* body undergoing the sacred *Rascooarno*, the developing soul must get into a state called "searching-for-some-other-similar-two-natured-arising-corresponding-to-itself" so that when the *Kesdjan* body within which it exists undergoes the sacred *Rascooarno*, it can "instantly enter this other body *Kesdjan* and continue to exist in it for its further perfection, which perfection must sooner or later be inevitably accomplished by every arisen higher being-body." These processes are called the "*Okipkhalevnian*-exchange-of-the-external-part-of-the-soul" or the "exchange-of-the-former-being-body-*Kesdjan*." Because the soul is composed of crystallizations received directly from the *Theomertmalogos*, or Word-God, it can never decompose and must exist in the given solar system where it has arisen until it can exist independently of the body *Kesdjan*.

Each of the three higher being-bodies is composed of very fine material. To acquire a soul, therefore, it is necessary to have the corresponding matter. Gurdjieff tells us that human beings, as three-brained beings, "can, by the conscious and intentional fulfilling of *being-Partkdolg-duty* . . . become such individuals as have their own sacred law of *Triamazikamno* [the *Law of Three* or the *Law of World Creation*, explained below], and thereby the possibility of consciously taking in and coating in their common presence all the 'Holy' which, incidentally, also aids the actualizing of the functioning in these cosmic units of Objective or Divine Reason."

As we are now, we lack enough energy even for our everyday functions. To have the material necessary for the growth of these bodies requires that we economize so that we have the energy for self-development. The aim is to crystallize these materials into the higher bodies. Gurdjieff explains,

> If we have some crystals of salt and put them in a glass of water, they will quickly dissolve. More can be added over and over again, and they will still dissolve. But there comes a moment when the solution is saturated. Then the salt no longer dissolves and the crystals remain whole on the bottom.
>
> It is the same with the human organism. Even if the materials which are required for the formation of a soul are being constantly produced in the organism, they are dispersed and dissolved in it. There must be a surfeit of such materials in the organism; only then is crystallization possible.
>
> The material crystallized after such a surfeit takes the form of the man's physical body, is a copy of it and may be separated from the physical body. Each body has a different life and each is subject to different orders of laws.

The materiality of these bodies and the development and purpose of the soul must be examined within the context of the universe or Megalocosmos.

The Megalocosmos & Our Role in It

Gurdjieff tells us that the universe came into existence when the Creator God established certain processes or laws that enabled Him to master time. It is these same laws that led to our creation, so we must understand and apply these laws for our own self-transformation and the development of our soul. As Gurdjieff states, "Man is an image of the world. He was created by the same laws which created the whole of the world [the Megalocosmos]. By knowing and understanding himself he will know and understand the whole world, all the laws that create and govern the world." Each of us "to the smallest detail is exactly similar, but of course in miniature, to the whole of our Megalocosmos." It is for this reason that we need to acquire self-knowledge, including an understanding of how these laws function within us, to develop our soul. To understand these laws, we must begin at the beginning, as Gurdjieff describes in *All and Everything*.

In the beginning, the Creator God existed on the Holy Sun Absolute surrounded only by empty, endless space. Yet space was not entirely empty; it was filled with the presence of the prime-source cosmic substance Etherokrilno, which is the basis for the "arising and maintenance of everything existing." The planets and suns did not yet exist. The Creator God came to realize that the Holy Sun Absolute was gradually diminishing. The Holy Sun Absolute existed on the basis of the Autoegocratic system; that is, it was a self-enclosed entity, existing independently and seemingly subject to no outside influence. But with time, it was subject to entropy and would eventually be destroyed. The Creator God did not know this; He had to discover it, and when He did, He "devoted HIMSELF entirely to finding a possibility of averting such an inevitable end."

The Creator God created the *Megalocosmos* by changing the system from the *Autoegocrat* to the *Trogoautoegocrat*—that is, requiring an exchange of substances or reciprocal feeding among everything existing, including, when they arose, human beings. The creation of the various worlds is referred to as the Ray of Creation. (*See* figure 1).

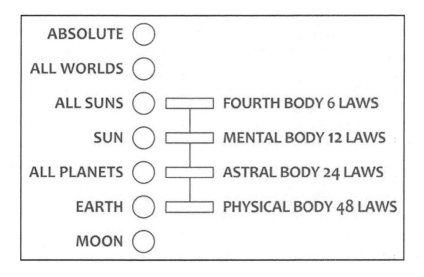

Figure 1

Everything that exists has its source in the Holy Sun Absolute. As Patterson explains, Creation starts from within the Holy Sun Absolute to "successive levels of worlds known as the Ray of Creation. The farther a given world, and the beings inhabiting it, from the Most Holy Sun Absolute, the more dense, the slower the vibration, the less intelligent and less conscious. Nonetheless, everything is an expression of energy, of vibration, of force, but at *different* levels. Thus, every thing, every manifestation, is *relative* in terms of its potency." (Patterson, *The Deep Question of Energy*, The Gurdjieff Journal, #45 [Emphasis in original]). The list to the right of the Ray of Creation depicts what Patterson describes. It correlates the source of the material to each of the bodies. The Soul, the highest body, is made of material of the world of All Suns. It is under only six orders of laws. The fewer the laws, the greater the freedom. This material vibrates at a much higher rate than the material that makes up our physical body. Ouspensky, *In Search of the Miraculous*, 94.

Within this Trogoautoegocratic system exists the prime source element *Omnipresent-Active-Element-Okidanokh*, which is created from the blendings of Etherokrilno with emanations of the Most Holy Sun Absolute called *Theomertmalogos*, or Word-God. *Okidanokh*'s prime arising then is *outside* the Most Holy Sun Absolute. This Omnipresent-Active-Element-*Okidanokh* takes part in the formation of all that exists.

As human beings, we take part in this Trogoautoegocratic process by receiving *Okidanokh* through the three foods: physical food, air and impressions. Simply by living, we receive this energy and transmit it. But we do so mechanically. That is, we eat, breathe, see and feel automatically; only occasionally are we aware of the intake of these foods.

It is only when we practice self-sensing and self-remembering, and so connect the three centers, that the *Okidanokh* contained in these foods undergoes *Djartklom*, a dividing of *Okidanokh* into three forces—active, passive, reconciling. These then blend, nourish and coat the three brains of our centers—intellectual, feeling, and instinctive—mixing with "kindred vibrations," which are localized in the corresponding brain. These blendings are known as *being-Impulsakri*, and it is the quality of these blendings that allows the self-perfecting and coating of the various bodies. If we do not practice *being-Partkdolg-duty*, then there is no *Djartklom*; and of the three brains, only the denying-brain in the spine is fed. Hence, if there is no conscious work, then the older one becomes, the more denying, the less conscious. However, "if the process [*Djartklom*] is conscious, activated through one's conscious labors and intentional sufferings . . . this effort results in 'the possibility personally to perfect' ourselves to possess a soul and the forging of Divine Reason."

Thus, we have a role to play in the maintenance of the universe, for within each of us "are all those separate functionings, which in our common Megalocosmos actualize the cosmic harmonious . . . 'exchange of substances,' maintaining the existence of everything existing in the Megalocosmos as one whole." We can fulfill our role unconsciously and "die like dogs," as Gurdjieff says, or we can fulfill our role consciously and also transform ourselves by working to grow a soul.

Techniques & Practices: The Megalocosmos within Us

As we are now, we are bioplasmic machines, reacting to internal and external stimuli in accordance with our programming. We are not the individual I that we think we are. Instead, we are many "I"s over which we have little control. Just as we are not the individual we take ourselves to be, we do not possess an immortal soul. We are soulless beings. Yet we have the possibility of developing a soul and so becoming fully developed images of God.

That is because, as three-brained beings that function like the *Megalocosmos*, we can consciously engage in our own law of creation, the Law of Three or *Triamazikamno*, and transform substances that help develop higher being-bodies. In our head-brain, we have cosmic substances corresponding to the functioning of the Absolute, which serve as the affirming source for developing within us our higher being-bodies. The denying source is located on the spinal column. The reconciling source is located in our solar plexus. As Gurdjieff tells a student, "The center of gravity of your presence is in your solar plexus, which is the center of feeling. That is where things happen." By consciously engaging in our own law of creation—that is, by engaging in *being-Partkdolg-duty*—we take in impressions consciously, enabling the finer substances that enter within us to transform and help develop higher being-bodies.

This requires work with the body. By engaging in the twin practices of *self-remembering* and *self-observation*, which begin with *self-sensing*, we can consciously relate to the physical body and the three centers—thinking, feeling, and moving/instinctive—and gradually become balanced so that no one center is dominant. And we take in impressions—what we eat, breathe, see, and feel—consciously, enabling the *Okidanokh* contained in these foods to divide into three forces, active, passive and reconciling, and coat our three centers.

Working consciously with the physical body and engaging in self-remembering and self-observation, we come to three-centered presence again and again. By doing so, we integrate and heat the finer substances and increase the sensation of the cells and tissues of the physical body so that a *Kesdjan* body begins to form, and we have the potential to develop a soul. In this internal process of creation, consciousness also grows, as does Objective Reason. The degree of one's consciousness or being correlates with the degree of one's Objective Reason.[12] If we fully develop higher being-bodies, we have a corresponding reason or intelligence, so that when we undergo death and leave the physical body, our higher being-bodies may be of assistance to the enlarging world in accordance with God's plan.

The Fourth Way practices of self-sensing, self-remembering and self-observation are the esoteric keys to spiritual transformation. But to access these practices in any meaningful way requires a teacher. As Gurdjieff says, we cannot teach ourselves, for who, what "I", is teaching us?

Conclusion

The teaching Gurdjieff brings is a sacred science of being that explains our place in the universe, as well as our responsibility to work to develop a soul and so participate consciously in the *Megalocosmos*. While the teaching is complex, the key components of the practice may be summarized in simple terms. The practice begins with an understanding that we are not born with an immortal soul, but we do have the possibility of creating one. The process of making a soul requires the wish to Be, to develop consciousness and the will to engage in a serious and sustained practice in order to attain the self-knowledge necessary for spiritual transformation.

Each of us must recognize for ourselves that I am not who I think am. I am not an Individual—that is, a unified I—but in reality am

---

[12] There are three kinds of being-reason. The first or highest is "pure" or objective being-reason, and it, rather than the physical body, is the "center-of-gravity-initiator-of-the-individual-functioning" of the whole presence of those who have attained to the corresponding level of being. The second being-reason can be in the presences of those who have a body-*Kesdjan*. The third being-reason is simply the "automatic functioning which proceeds in the common presences of all beings in general . . . thanks to repeated shocks from outside, which evoke habitual reactions from the data crystallized in them corresponding to previous accidentally perceived impressions." Teresa Adams, "Gurdjieff and Pythagoras—The Hyperborean Apollo," Part II, *The Gurdjieff Journal*, Vol. 18, No. 2, 11.

composed of many "I"s with different needs, desires and perspectives that take over in mechanical reaction to a given situation or stimulus. This is to be verified through our own lived experience.

The practices and techniques all begin with the body. The esoteric key to which the ancient sages allude is literally right beneath our noses. It is the practice of *self-remembering* and *self-observation,* which begins with *self-sensing*—that is, redirecting the attention out of our head and our mechanical, associative thoughts and into the physical body, where we maintain a conscious, present awareness of the physical sensation of the body. Over time, we develop a global awareness of the body and of what is occurring internally, as well as externally.

Through the sustained practice of *being-Partkdolg-duty,* the conscious labors and intentional sufferings that take place when we observe ourselves *impartially* in conscious awareness, we suffer the truth of the many contradictory "I"s, steeped in self-love and vanity, that make up our false personality and control our behavior. Gradually, with continued efforts, we begin to integrate these many "I"s, taking back their power to control us and developing real will.

Engaging in these practices and techniques, finer and finer substances accumulate within us, and we begin to develop a *Kesdjan* body, which leads to the possibility of developing a soul. As consciousness grows, so does Objective Reason—that is, a knowledge of the All grounded in self-knowledge. This process takes many years of sincere and sustained effort.

Only by awakening to your wish for self-transformation and transcendence will you have the opportunity to verify the teaching. That is, only through conscious labors and intentional sufferings, *being-Partkdolg-duty,* can you crystallize the finer materials necessary for developing the higher being-bodies and create a soul. The Fourth Way is a scientific method of developing and growing a soul—its esoteric practices are precise and the experiences are definite, not imaginary, with nothing to be believed and everything to be verified. The Fourth Way is the teaching for our time. By engaging in the teaching, we can in fact awaken to our mechanicality and be open to the realization that we are indeed an image of God. In short, The Fourth Way provides those seeking spiritual transformation a true path to develop Conscience, Consciousness and Being—to grow a soul.

CHAPTER TWO

ANCIENT EGYPT

The Universe is nothing but Consciousness, and in all its appearances reveals nothing but an evolution of Consciousness, from its origin to its end, which is a return to its cause. It is the goal of every "initiatory" religion to teach the way to this ultimate union.

—R.A. Schwaller de Lubicz

IN GURDJIEFF'S QUEST FOR KNOWLEDGE, HE TRAVELED TO EGYPT AND FOLLOWED THE NILE TO ITS SOURCE IN ABYSSINIA. GURDJIEFF WAS INITIATED FOUR TIMES INTO THE EGYPTIAN MYSTERIES. The Fourth Way teaching that Gurdjieff brought to the West, with its emphasis on the need to develop a soul, had its origins in Egypt. Here we will explore what can be known of the ancient Egyptian teaching, which Gurdjieff reformulated for modern times.

While Western thought examines questions concerning the creation and ramifications of the soul through a philosophical or a religious lens, the ancient Egyptians did so by means of what eminent Egyptologist R. A. Schwaller de Lubicz called "sacred science." Egyptians knew the soul not through theories or ideas to be taken on faith but rather through practices leading to the soul's development and growth.

The key understanding of the Egyptians was that our soul is only a potentiality—which we must develop and grow. [13]

The difficulty with appreciating the wisdom that the Egyptians attained is that their sacred science devolved. What we have been left with are images of Egyptian art, misunderstood in modern times as naive and merely depicting animal worship. However, if we can dispel those notions, there is great value in considering the knowledge of the ancient Egyptians through a new perspective.

Ancient Egyptian Knowledge & Symbology

Studying the ancient Egyptians through this new perspective is a process that requires a mode of thinking that is different from the typical Western mentality, which de Lubicz refers to as "cerebral consciousness." Cerebral thinking is comparative, registering the new and limiting it by weighing it against what is known. It's possible that's what you've been doing while reading this book. When we are confronted with something novel, we tend to "obey our reductionist tendency and restrict both the cause and the phenomenon to the realm of the mechanical mentality." However, "reality," de Lubicz said, "reveals itself through the esoteric sense of synthesis, the vital link of which is broken and rejected by a cerebral analysis that only leaves parts isolated from each other, and from which it is impossible for mechanistic determinism to approach the secret of life." Thus, the Egyptian mentality was indirect and speaks to an inner vision, treating the part only in relation to the spirit of the whole to which it belongs. This vision comes through what the Egyptians referred to as "the intelligence of the heart," in stark contrast to cerebral analysis.

---

[13] The original belief was that pharaohs were the only ones born with a soul. Patterson, *Gurdjieff in Egypt*, DVD; also Isha Schwaller de Lubicz, *The Opening of the Way: A Practical Guide to the Wisdom of Ancient Egypt* (Rochester, VT: Inner Traditions, 1981), 203. Isha Schwaller de Lubicz, *Her-Bak: Egyptian Initiate* (New York: Inner Traditions, 1979), 360–61. See also *Spiritism and the Cult of the Dead in Antiquity*, Lewis Bayles Paton (New York: MacMillan, 1921), 155, 175, 177.

The Egyptians' knowledge of the method and purpose of spiritual development is conveyed by the imagery, hieroglyphs, temples, and monuments they left behind. These structures date back to eras well before the first pharaonic dynasties of about 3100 BCE. One of ancient Egypt's many remarkable features was its stability; it was a civilization that retained the same language, writing, symbols, and religion for tens of thousands of years.[14] De Lubicz, recognizing that we tend to lower what we see to our own level, eschewed the assumption of many that Egypt's stability was simply a reflection of a stagnant society incapable of evolving. Rather, he argues that Egypt's stability stemmed from its achievement of realizing the ultimate aim of all knowledge—to liberate oneself from the perishable—and thus no further evolution could be expected.

The employment of forms and symbols by the ancient Egyptian temple builders was not an effort to hide the truth; rather it was an effort to reveal the truth to those who had, through initiation, developed the necessary understanding. What was being revealed, de Lubicz said, was knowledge concerning the laws of life by an elite who possessed this knowledge. What we see in Egyptian symbology is a synthesis of a world of causes. The word de Lubicz preferred was the French word *symbolique*, referring to the concrete image of a synthesis that cannot otherwise be expressed in time or in comprehensible dimensions. These are principles or *neters* conveyed symbolically as gods. The gods in ancient Egypt were in fact principles, incarnations of cosmic functions; they were essentially verbs, not nouns. Thus de Lubicz's use of the term

---

[14] The Royal Papyrus of Turin, which was discovered in 1820 in Luxor (ancient city of Thebes), lists the dynasties preceding Menes's reign and the duration of each dynasty. Menes is the pharaoh who was credited with founding the First Dynasty after uniting Upper and Lower Egypt. There is widespread variation among scholars as to when this dynasty originated. Some put it at about 3100 BCE; de Lubicz posits that the Menes Dynasty could have begun as early as 4240 BCE; Jean-François Champollion asserted it began even earlier, c. 5860 BCE. In any event, the nine dynasties preceding Menes's account for over 36,000 years, the last of which was that of the Shemsu-Hor, meaning the "Companions of Horus." Its reign alone lasted over 13,000 years. De Lubicz, *Sacred Science: The King of Pharaonic Theocracy* (Rochester, VT: Inner Traditions, 1988), 86.

symbolique is a means of evoking the intuition of a function that eludes rationalization. By way of example, de Lubicz speaks of a depiction of the hand extended, a gesture of *giving* with the palm opened downward or *receiving* with palm upward, as aspects of the human totality. It is the gesture that conveys the action of receiving or giving, rather than the specific function depicted in its limited sense—the giving or receiving of *something*. Instead, it symbolizes an exchange, perhaps an exchange of energies. To be able to use *symbolique* practically requires either a rational system of interpretation, which the Egyptians shunned as an exoteric approach, or the application of one's innate knowledge. The type of knowledge to which this refers is self-knowledge. Thus, one's level of understanding grows with one's being and self-knowledge.

Looking at what the Egyptians left behind in their sacred temples, we are seeing "not the beginnings of research, but the application of knowledge already possessed." That knowledge reveals the Egyptian understanding of the purpose of life and the importance of the soul, which represented the immortal principle. "Through its figurations, the teachings of Pharaonic Egypt become a marvelous history which speaks of what has always been, what always shall be the essential knowledge concerning origin, aim and finality of life." Yet the difficulty of learning from the ancient Egyptians is that "there has never been a greater distance between consciousnesses than there is in our time between Western mentality and the mentality of the ancient Egyptian sages." As de Lubicz rhetorically asks, "The error of our world, is it not that of not knowing how to read the Universe as a concrete symbol of the abstract sense of the functional powers which govern it?"

The Egyptians understood that the universe is nothing but consciousness and that the aim of life is to integrate with consciousness. The ancient name for Egypt was "Kemi," and the Arabs called Egypt "Al-Kemi" (in the West, alchemy), a reference to the principle that matter as a field of existence is responsive to and capable of being transformed by spiritual influences brought about "through the evolution of embodied and individualized consciousness." Thus, their sacred science shows us the way to move from complexity to extreme simplicity.

Man's Relation to the Cosmos

The vision of anthropocosmos sees man as being and containing within himself the entire universe. The Egyptian perspective was that anthropocosmos was a reality, a foundation from which all true knowledge comes. It is based on the understanding that "we have nothing to discover outside ourselves." Humanity is the living expression of the whole of divine thought.

The Egyptians brought this vision to life in the Temple of Man, an initiatory temple located in Thebes, modern-day Luxor. Its construction was begun in the fourteenth century BCE by the pharaoh Amenhotep III and dedicated to the sun god Amon-Re. It is a study of the human body portraying the vital functions of the organs leading to "the inevitable resurrection of the spiritual essence which has involved itself in matter in the form of organic creative energy." It teaches that this resurrection is accomplished through the transformation of matter:

> The birth of divine man (symbolized by the pharaoh) depends upon the transformation of the universal mother (materia prima). This transformation was considered the sole cosmic goal. Every human birth participates in this alchemy, either in an awakened manner through the intentional perfecting and expression of one's higher nature, or unawakened, through the tumult and suffering of karmic experience leading eventually to a spiritual self-awareness, the temple in man. The intensification and heightening of human consciousness was believed to cause biological and even cellular changes in the physical body of the initiate. This divinization of the individual body, on the microcosmic level, comprised the goal and purpose of the evolution of human consciousness in general.

Thus through "spiritual metabolism," humanity can liberate the energy or spirit manifested in the intellectual faculties and powers of consciousness. In this process, consciousness becomes integrated with the body and paradoxically becomes independent of the body: "The body itself becomes energy, being no longer the support of an energy, no longer the container but wholly the contents." The knowledge of how this is done was attributed to the *Shemsu-Hor*, "those who follow the path of Horus," who bore with them knowledge of divine origin. According to the Papyrus of Turin, they created the first Egyptian dynasty about 40,000 years ago and reigned in ancient Egypt for over 13,000 years. This is similar to what Gurdjieff says about the learned society of Akhaldans, who approached the acquisition of objective knowledge to a degree never before, or since. The word *Akhaldan* means "the striving to become aware of the sense and aim of the Being of beings." According to Gurdjieff, this society was formed on the continent Atlantis where it existed until Atlantis was engulfed. The Akhaldans, however, did not all perish; some sailed to what is now Africa and settled on the Nile. British Egyptologist W. B. Emery, in his 1961 book *Archaic Egypt*, supports the sudden development of the Egyptian culture, suggesting that it appeared out of nowhere. Although his time frames differ, he dates this sudden change from the close of the fourth millennium BCE; he likewise attributes the principal cause of this sudden cultural advance to "the incursion of new people into the Nile valley." He identifies these people as the "Followers of Horus," who formed a "master race ruling over the whole of Egypt."

R. A. Schwaller de Lubicz

Horus & Set

The path of Horus is depicted through myth. Understanding of myth leads to understanding of Self and the aim of human existence. At Delphi, it is written: *Man, know thyself and thou shalt know the universe and the gods.* As de Lubicz states, "This thought has served as the foundation for all revelations concerning the secret of becoming and the return of being to its source."

Egyptian mythology is told through the *neters*, the active principles that cause phenomena. A *neter* is a mode of action, a law of divine harmony, giving rise to forms and signatures and commanding the phases of becoming and returning to the source. It is not a participant in the action; rather it designates a mode of action. While the *neters* are anthropomorphized in Egyptian mythology, they are not humanized as with the Greek Olympian gods. *Neters* operate on both the human scale and the universal scale. On our level, the human body is an incarnation of these *neters*. One may become aware that one's qualities and knowledge are not personal to oneself but are imperfect reflections of the attributes of the Creator. This awareness takes place by awakening to the body and its functional identity with the *neters*.

The story of Horus, one of the greatest gods of Egyptian mythology, reveals the path toward the development of the soul and its return to the source. William Patrick Patterson explains the significance of this wisdom story employing the art and symbolism of the Temple of Edfu, which is dedicated to the god Horus. According to this myth, the first king of mankind was Horus's father, Osiris, who represents the creative principle. He brought mankind up from barbarism, giving us agriculture and the arts. However, the creative principle requires opposition for its fulfillment, and Set (or Seth), Osiris's brother and the Lord of Materiality and Carnality, provided the opposition necessary for cosmic creation. Set was jealous and killed Osiris, cutting him into pieces and scattering the pieces throughout Egypt. Osiris's wife, Isis, went in search of the pieces and found only his phallus. Osiris was so potent that he was able to impregnate Isis, leading to the birth of Horus, the first immaculate birth, foreshadowing Christianity's story of Jesus's birth. As Horus grew up, he struggled with his uncle and finally subjugated Set.

Patterson explains that in overcoming Set, Horus unites himself spiritually, the unification symbolized by the fact that in his battle with Set, Horus loses one eye, symbolically becoming an individual I. Set also loses something in the battle, a testicle, weakening carnal power and giving the spiritual principal the requisite sovereignty. Thus, Set represents opposition in the spiritual sense, playing the same role as Satan in the Judaic Christian tradition. Set, our material and carnal aspects, has a role in creating the necessary opposition for spiritual development. Through Horus's struggle with Set, he awakens to his true spiritual capabilities. However, Horus can never entirely defeat Set, because if he did, there would be no world. And if Horus were defeated, it would result in his being imprisoned in materiality and carnality, becoming no more than an animal.

In his struggle, Horus gains the native intelligence that was lost with his descent into matter, and the spiritual and material become reunited in a genuine way. Set becomes Horus's companion. The relationship becomes one of friendship. The Temple of Edfu, while dedicated to Horus—who is, after all, representative of a *neter*—is actually dedicated to the self-transformation of man. Horus enters the higher realms by means of acquired consciousness—universal soul surpassing nature. The Egyptians understood that man's corporeal life is not an end in itself but a transition. An eternal element takes on a corporeal form momentarily. The purpose of this existence is, through the engagement with oppositional forces, to evolve consciousness or being. Put another way, to grow a soul.

Historical references to the Egyptian king support this view. As Henri Frankfort writes in his book *Kingship and the Gods*, the king was referred to as "The Two Lords." He explains this as a reference that allows us to "touch upon more profound religious symbolism. 'The Two Lords' were the perennial antagonists, Horus and Seth. The king was identified with both of these gods, but not in the sense that he was considered the incarnation of one, and also the incarnation of the other. He embodied them as a pair, *as opposites in equilibrium.*" A pyramid text referencing the king's rebirth to eternal life again epitomizes the role of Horus and Seth: "Thou art born, [reborn] because of Horus (in thee) Thou art conceived because of Seth (in thee)." He further explains that this applied to the queen, whose ancient title was "She who sees

Horus-and-Seth," the implication of which is that she sees Horus and Seth in herself.

The followers of Horus were the temple elite. For the masses, there was the Osirian cult of renewal and reincarnation. The karmic consequences of reincarnation create a "wheel of exhaustion moving toward liberation. It is the law *for all*. Reincarnation is both punishment and a divine mercy that allows one to make amends." This may lead toward liberation—the conscious evolutionary end within a corporeal form.

Horus and Set

Growing a Soul

The approach to understanding the Egyptian perspective and experience of the soul begins by exploring what can be known of the principles that govern the creation of the universe. As noted, the Egyptians understood that the universe is consciousness from beginning to the end—with the end being a return to its cause. "The first stage is a decline of the sole Cause, primordial and indefinable, into the corporal." All that exists proceeds from this unnamed, limitless, and incomprehensible source or unity, *neter* of *neters*. Thus, creation is a process of division, not addition.

Within this primordial unity are three principles, also unnamable and designated simply by hieroglyphs *A*, *N*, and *H*. No one principle precedes the others, and while each has its properties, together they are a perfect unity. This is also the basis for the mystery of the Trinity spoken of in Christianity and what Gurdjieff refers to in The Fourth Way as the Law of Three, *Triamazikamno*. All creation stems from the interaction of three forces encompassed in the One.

The initial creative act that ultimately leads to the universe is revealed with the appearance of *Atum*, meaning both All and Nothing:

> This word serves to express at once *affirmation* (of existence) and the *negation* (of the original unity by the very fact of that creation). Accordingly, the word expresses being and non-being; non-being becomes the source, and being becomes its negation. This reversal of notions is typical of pharaonic thought.

What first emerges from the creative act is symbolized in Egyptian mythology by *Râ* (sun or solar light) rising out of *Nut* (sky). *Râ* symbolizes the attribute of creative activity, the solar spiritual principle. *Râ* is the first author of names at the beginning of things. He is portrayed as the light proceeding out of darkness.

The Egyptians called the Creator *Atum-Râ-Ptah*, the source of all being, whose image is within every human. The image referred to is not that of the person but of the three forces. Those who reunite the three forces of *Atum-Râ-Ptah* in consciousness are themselves unified. *Ptah* is the hidden drive in one's life, the active and causal principle—captive through his fall into matter. The heat of his activity is the source of all life symbolized in Egypt by fire. The world's prime matter is perpetually manufactured by *Ptah*, impersonal existence in and for itself; its only objective is existence.

The process of involution leading to the personal is recognized by *ikw*, signifying being into becoming with all its phases and turns of fortune. It is the cause of the fall into matter, creating duality and all that results from duality. Yet from duality the possibility exists of a new birth, the birth of a conscious human being who has acquired higher reason. The ancient Egyptians recognized that the main function of life is assimilation, and what they sought was the "Assimilation into the Divine."

Our mortal body is animated by *Ba*, which gives life and whose departure causes death. *Ba* is the second aspect of spirit, the "divine intermediary between heaven and earth." In human beings, as in all forms of life, *Ba* must have a support to manifest. That support is provided by the *Ka*, which allows the *Ba* to become individualized. *Ka* is the creative principle of fixation and attraction, giving form to matter. Both *Ba* and *Ka* emerge from *ia*, the causal principle of breath, the first aspect of the one and only spirit, *iaaw*.

Thus, we are composed of a mortal physical body and have within us undeveloped immortal elements; we might think of them as the seeds of possibilities. *Ba* is in everything, and it has three aspects: the cosmic soul, natural soul—which stabilizes in bodily form—and human soul. Like the *Ba*, *Ka* has three aspects:

- original *Ka*, creator of all other forms
- *Ka* of humanity
- *Ka* of nature—including the mineral, vegetable, and animal

Ka is the source of creation of all matter, from the lowest of forms to the indestructible, perfected body. Isha Schwaller de Lubicz employs this helpful metaphor toward understanding the *Ka*: "It is hard to distinguish the different aspects of the *Ka*, because their difference lies not in their source or cause, [for there is only one source] but only in their effects. If the light of the sun is reflected by several mirrors made of different metals, it will take on different colors and qualities . . . Each [*Ka*] is characterized in the man to whom it is incarnated, by the signatures of the vital forces (the natural, organic, and instinctive *Kas*) which it finds in him, and by the innate consciousness of his being."

Ka is also the agent of our consciousness, whose source is what the Egyptians called Maât. Thus, "*Ba* in relation to *Ka* is the animating spirit. *Ka*, in relation to *Ba*, is the individualization of consciousness." The higher qualities of *Ka* only become incorporated within us when we acquire knowledge and mastery over them. Through this process we may assimilate the cosmic *Ba*, enabling our *Ka* to generate a new being—the individualized, immortal soul. Upon the death of the mortal body, the *Ba* may be prepared for a final liberation into *Maât*-consciousness; if not, it again incarnates to continue on the path toward becoming conscious.

The Egyptians likened the created human body to a net in which the soul is enmeshed:

> Although the function of the body was to sustain life, this was not considered the body's ultimate goal; rather, it was to act as a net in which its Hidden Dweller—the soul—is caught as a prey and ultimately exalted. This exaltation of the soul is a mystical, irrational process. The net and its prey are really one being.

The human soul moves between heaven and earth to range about the body until the purification of the *Ka-djet (djet* being the subtle, indestructible, or incorruptible body) allows the body to incorporate the soul. This purification leads to consciousness of all *neters*, the divine powers and principles manifesting in nature and thus within each of us. Through this purification, we become masters of ourselves as we become *masters of neters*. One Egyptian depiction of the *Ba* employing the body of a bird with a human head symbolizes the "struggle on the part of the dead man's higher consciousness to be free of the lower elements that haunt it 'like a Shade.' It is in fact through this Shade that he is involved in struggles that [both] delay [and make possible] reunion of the higher *Ka* with the *Ba*. For the divine soul, *Ba*, can only be held by a man's particular *Ka* in an incorruptible body when all that is foreign to it, corruptible, has been eliminated."

The obstacles to purification begin at birth. Once a child is born, the *Ka* arouses a personal urge that becomes *Me* (the Egyptian word

Me is an appropriate coincidence), the basis of which is the principle of egoism, which grows with the child, crystallizing the *Ka*'s tendencies to its own advantage, to affirm its existence and assure its continuity. This *Me* is what deludes us about the importance of our own thoughts, which are nothing but a play of ephemeral forces and relative values—not a causal power but an effect. The *Me* is neither the body nor any of the spiritual factors. Though the *Me* arises through the incarnation of a spiritual being, it seeks to absorb the inclinations and appetites that belong to the *Ka*'s affinities.

The *Me* stands in stark contrast to the *Ka*. The *Ka* is the only aspect through which immortality can be gained, possessing an affinity to the forces that created it. The *Me* is absorbed by what is agreeable to its egoism, creating for each of us a "mass of impure and destructible factors that hinder possession of" our *Ka* on earth and reunion with the *Ka* in the *Dwat* (the netherworld). The *Me*'s desire for personal existence loses its potency as we acquire self-knowledge, consciousness that our true being is a functional identity with the *neters*. The *Ka* thus assimilates *Ba* and generates a new being, another body, the individualized soul, "divine, incorruptible, immortal, yet conditioned by the acquired affinity with the *Ka*'s particularity."

The higher *Ka* is not of nature and is not embodied in an ordinary person, who is controlled only by the lower *Ka*, which includes the "signatures and the innate and acquired characteristics of personality and all passionate, psychic and organic animal impulses." Human beings have a higher *Ka*—that is, our spiritual entity—which descends from *Maât* (cosmic consciousness).

> The higher *Ka* ... will become incarnate only if consciousness develops sufficient independence to give mastery over the lower *Ka* to the individual. Ancient Egypt insistently offers men this aim: to achieve "conscious union of both *Ka* so as to awaken the higher human reason and allow intuitive knowledge to be connected with ideas."
>
> The divine element of man can then become fixed. The divine *Ba*, his Horian soul, when attracted by the fulfilled total *Ka*, forms a union that is the ultimate promise of immortality.

Conclusion

So to sum up what we have seen about Egypt's sacred science, the Egyptians understood that our soul is only a potentiality—which we must develop and grow. Within our mortal physical body, we have undeveloped immortal elements. Development of these elements is possible through the integration of our consciousness with the universal consciousness. The intensification and heightening of human consciousness causes biological and even cellular changes in our physical body.

Our body is animated by *Ba*, which gives life and is supported by *Ka*, allowing the *Ba* to become individualized. *Ka* is the creative principle of fixation and attraction, giving form to matter. All that exists, including the *Ba* and the *Ka*, proceeds from the unnamed, limitless, and incomprehensible source, or Unity. In addition to being the principle of fixation and attraction, *Ka* is also the agent of our consciousness, whose source is what the Egyptians called Maât. The higher qualities of *Ka* only become incorporated within us when we acquire knowledge and mastery over them. Through this process, we may assimilate the *cosmic Ba* (the highest of the three *Ba*), enabling our *Ka* to generate a new being—the individualized, immortal soul.

Gurdjieff tells us that all the great genuine religions are based on the same truths. As these religions are concerned not with dogma, but with the growth and development of Being, all are intended to help us fulfill our purpose as human beings through the growth of self-knowledge. Gurdjieff put it this way: "The difference in those religions is only in the definite regulations they lay down for the *observance of certain details* and of what are called rituals; and this difference is the result of the deliberate adoption by the great founders of these regulations which suited the degree of the mental perfection of the people of the given period."

We have now seen the esoteric connection between Gurdjieff's teaching of The Fourth Way and the religion of prehistoric Egypt. We will explore further how the same truths are set forth in a surprising source: Christianity. Not the Christianity that we commonly know, but the little known *esoteric* Christianity that teaches about the possibilities of developing and growing a soul. In the following chapters, we will explore and compare Christianity's exoteric and the esoteric teachings on the soul and see how esoteric Christianity is based on the same truths found in prehistoric Egypt and Gurdjieff's teaching of The Fourth Way.

CHAPTER THREE

CHRISTIANITY

IT IS OFTEN A SURPRISE TO THOSE RAISED AS CHRISTIANS TO LEARN THAT THE CHRISTIAN THEOLOGY OF THE SOUL IS NOT BASED ON THE FOUR GOSPELS THAT FORM THE CHRISTIAN CANON. Rather, the idea of the soul developed over the course of centuries, with the early church fathers initially rejecting the notion of an immortal soul inhabiting the corporeal body. Despite this initial rejection, the many forms of contemporary Christianity, from Roman Catholicism to Eastern Orthodox to mainstream Protestant denominations to Evangelical sects, now share in the fundamental belief that each human being is endowed with an immortal soul; that Jesus Christ was the son of God who came to earth, was crucified to redeem humankind of its sins,[15] and was resurrected from the dead; and that belief in Jesus Christ provides salvation and eternal life for immortal souls in heaven. This belief in an immortal

---

[15] There are important theological differences between Roman Catholicism and the Protestant religions that developed from it, and the teachings of the Eastern Orthodox Church. Significantly, Eastern Orthodox theology does not view Christ's crucifixion as redeeming the original sin of Adam shared by all human beings but rather as a triumph over death and the powers of evil. *See* Timothy Ware, *The Orthodox Church: New Edition* (London: Penguin Books, 2nd ed., 1997), 224–29. However, the crucifixion and resurrection of Jesus are integral to the Orthodox teaching that all human beings have an immortal soul.

soul is also tied to belief in the resurrection, which some denominations hold will be a bodily resurrection, while others understand it to be a resurrection of the soul itself at the end of time or the Day of Judgment. Variations on this core teaching are innumerable, but the belief in the immortal soul is now universal within Christianity.

It may also come as a surprise that the Christian theology of the soul cannot be traced directly to the words of Jesus Christ as recorded in the New Testament. Instead, it developed as part of an ongoing conflict among the early church fathers over numerous aspects of Christian teaching. As recorded in the four Gospels of Matthew, Mark, Luke, and John that ultimately became the canon of the New Testament, the teachings of the historical Jesus make relatively few references to the word *soul*, and those that He makes are ambiguous. The Gnostic Gospels, which were considered heresy by the early church fathers, include statements of Jesus and a variety of teachings that provide a more expansive treatment of the soul.

Jesus Christ (Cathedral of Cefalù, Sicily)

It was the teachings of Paul of Tarsus, however, that most profoundly shaped the future doctrines of the Roman Catholic Church on the soul, particularly those of Augustine and Thomas Aquinas, the two most influential theologians of the premodern period who will be discussed in chapter four. And as we will see in chapter five, with accurate translation, it is also possible to read Paul's teachings in a very different light, as *esoteric* teachings that reveal a theology of the soul with strong parallels to that brought by Gurdjieff at the beginning of the 20th century.

The Soul in the Gospels of the New Testament

The first three gospels in the New Testament—Matthew, Mark, and Luke—are called the Synoptic Gospels because they include many of the same stories.[16] The Gospel of John, written much later, has significantly distinct content. Modern biblical historians agree that all four Gospels are anonymous writings assigned names as titles to distinguish them by later church leaders, not as recognition of their authors. And while the order and dating of the four Gospels have been studied and debated for centuries, many contemporary biblical scholars believe they were most likely written sometime between the late first century, after the destruction of Jerusalem in 70 CE, to the mid-second century, up to a hundred years after the death of Jesus. The four Gospels quote Jesus speaking only sparingly about the soul, and in them Jesus provides no detailed teaching on the soul. Nor does He state explicitly that all human beings have a soul. In fact, the incidences in which Jesus is depicted as referencing the soul are so few that most of them can be addressed in a short section below.

Preliminarily, it should be noted that the New Testament was originally written in Greek. A variety of meanings inhere to the Greek word for *soul*. The word originally meant "breath, life breath, or the principle of life." It also suggested physical life or a living being and sometimes meant the seat of eternal life or, alternatively, the seat of desires, feelings, and emotions. Thus all references to *soul* in the New Testament must be read in context to discern the meaning behind the

---

[16] The word *synoptic* comes from the Greek *syn*, meaning "together," and *optic*, meaning "seen."

word. And variations in modern translations heighten the ambiguity, with the word *soul* often used interchangeably with the words *life* or *I* in different translations.

The first reference to the soul in the New Testament is in Matthew, which scholars agree was written after Mark, although it precedes Mark in the scriptures. In Matthew 10:28, Jesus distinguishes the soul from the body when comforting the disciples as they face persecution: "Do not fear those who kill the body but are unable to kill the soul; but rather, fear Him who is able to destroy both body and soul in hell." By juxtaposing the "soul" to the "life" of the body, the quote clearly refers to a soul that is something more than "life-giving breath." The passage also suggests that the soul is not necessarily immortal, as it may be destroyed in hell.

In Matthew, when Jesus admonishes the disciples to take up the cross and follow Him, He tells them, "For what will it profit a man if he gains the whole world and forfeits his soul? Or what will a man give in exchange for his soul?" Modern translations of this quote in Matthew, as well as the parallel verse found in Mark, replace the word *soul* with *life*; in the parallel verse found in Luke, the words *self* or *himself* are used in place of *soul*. In another reference to the soul, Matthew quotes from the Old Testament book of Isaiah, traditionally translated as "Behold, my servant whom I have chosen; my beloved in whom my soul is well-pleased; I will put my spirit upon him, and he shall proclaim justice to all the gentiles." Matthew also quotes Jesus as suggesting that His teachings can restore the soul: "Come to me, all who are weary and heavy-laden, and I will give you rest. Take my yoke upon you and learn from me, for I am gentle and humble in heart, and you will find rest for your souls." There are no parallel quotes in Mark and Luke for either of these passages.

When asked which commandment is the greatest, Jesus answers in Matthew:

> You shall love the Lord your God
> with all your heart,
> and with all your soul,
> and with all your mind.

In Mark, the words "and with all your strength" are added to this quote. The quote appears in Luke as part of the introduction to the parable of the Good Samaritan, as Jesus answers the question, "What shall I do to inherit eternal life?" These quotes distinguish among the terms *body, heart, soul,* and *mind,* a distinction that can be traced back to the Greeks, but no definition or further clarification of the terms is given in the Gospels.

There are references to the soul in Luke that do not appear in the other Gospels. For example, Luke tells us that when Mary, pregnant with Jesus, visits her cousin Elizabeth, who is carrying John the Baptist, Elizabeth proclaims that the baby leaped for joy in her womb. Mary responds, "My soul exalts the Lord, and my spirit has rejoiced in God my Savior." And in the parable of the rich fool, when a rich man decides to build larger barns to store his grain and goods, he declares,

> I will say to my soul, "Soul, you have many goods laid up for many years to come; take your ease, eat, drink, be merry." But God said to him, "You fool! This *very* night your soul is required of you; and *now* who will own what you have prepared?"

In many translations of this parable, the word *soul,* as used by the rich fool, is replaced with "myself" and "you," and God tells the rich fool his "life" will be required, rather than his "soul."

All four Gospels tell the story of Jesus in the garden of Gethsemane the night before the crucifixion, in which He prays to be relieved of what is to come. In Matthew and Mark, the story is almost identical, with Jesus first telling the apostles, "My soul is deeply grieved, to the point of death; remain here and keep watch with me," and then moving away from them to pray, "let this cup pass from me." Luke portrays the same scene, but without Jesus referencing the anguish of His soul. In John, Jesus is quoted as saying, "Now my soul has become troubled; and what shall I say, 'Father, save me from this hour'? But for this purpose I came to this hour." Interestingly, the various translations of Matthew, Mark and John use the word *soul* in these verses almost universally; it is rarely translated as "*I* am grieved." Of course, the notion that Jesus possesses a soul would surprise no one.

Perhaps for this reason, the depiction of Gethsemane is the only direct reference to the "soul" that can be found in John. The Gospel of John developed separately from the Synoptic Gospels. Only about eight percent of its content is parallel to the stories in the Synoptic Gospels, and there is no mention of some of the most famous of biblical stories, including the Last Supper, the Sermon on the Mount and the Lord's Prayer. Instead, it begins with Jesus Christ as a preexisting deity, "the Word [made] flesh," and focuses on the "glorified Christ," as Jesus is portrayed in the writings of Paul. Although there is only one reference to the soul, there are a number of references to "eternal life" and "resurrection" in John that suggest the concept of an immortal soul. For example, it is in John that we find the verse "For God so loved the world, that He gave His only begotten Son, that whoever believes in Him shall not perish, but have eternal life." In John, Jesus states, "Truly, truly, I say to you, he who hears My word, and believes Him who sent Me, has eternal life, and does not come into judgment, but has passed out of death into life." Similarly, Jesus states, "I am the living bread that came down out of heaven; if anyone eats of this bread, he will live forever; and the bread also which I will give for the life of the world is My flesh."

Regarding the resurrection, in John there is a depiction of Jesus comforting Martha after the crucifixion, in which He says to her, "I am the resurrection and the life; he who believes in Me will live even if he dies, and everyone who believes in Me will never die." And John has Jesus telling a gathering of followers, "Do not marvel at this; for an hour is coming, in which all who are in the tombs will hear His voice, and will come forth; those who did the good deeds to a resurrection of life, those who committed the evil deeds to a resurrection of judgment."

Similarly, in Matthew and Mark, Jesus responds to a question about the afterlife regarding a woman who was married seven times:

> For in the resurrection they neither marry nor are given in marriage, but are like angels in heaven.

Finally, there is a scene portrayed in Luke not found in the other Gospels that suggests the existence of an immortal soul. At the crucifixion, Luke depicts a conversation between Jesus and one of the two thieves also being crucified.

> And he was saying, "Jesus, remember me when You come in Your kingdom." And He said to him, "Truly I say to you, today you shall be with Me in Paradise."

As can be seen from this brief review, there are not many references to the soul in the four Gospels that make up the canon of the Christian scriptures, nor is there a definition or theology of the soul. And when used, the word *soul* is often interchanged in modern translations of the ancient Greek with the words *I*, *life*, *spirit* and *heart*, depending on the context. Nevertheless, the passages cited above are some of the most oft-quoted within Christian theology and incorporated into Christian services, and historically they were translated using the word *soul*. These passages, coupled with references to "eternal life" and "resurrection" in the four Gospels and in the writings of Paul, became the foundation of the Christian teaching on the immortality of the soul.

Paul—The Thirteenth Apostle

Although the New Testament begins with the writings of Matthew, Mark, Luke and John, the first Christian writings were actually the letters of Paul, sometimes referred to as the "Thirteenth Apostle." Paul wrote in the mid-first century, sometime between 50 and 68 CE, *before* the canonical Gospels were written and well before they were chosen by the church fathers as the scriptures of the New Testament. Paul never met Jesus, and according to his own letters was frequently at odds with Peter and James, the leaders of the twelve apostles who Jesus chose to preach His gospel. Yet Paul's thirteen letters and the story of his missionary works in the Acts of the Apostles dominate the New Testament canon, and it is Paul's version of Christianity that became the foundation of Christian theology—the key tenets of orthodox teachings not only on the soul and the resurrection but on topics ranging from politics to sex to the role of women in the church. Some scholars have gone so far as to argue that Paul was the "founder" of Christianity, his teachings having triumphed not only over the Gnostic teachings of other gospels but also over the teachings of the original leaders of the nascent Christian religion—Peter, James and John. For example, James D. Tabor, a professor of religious studies and author of *Paul and Jesus: How the Apostle Transformed Christianity*, argues that the foundational doctrinal tenets of Christianity—that Christ is God "born in the flesh," that His sacrificial death atones for the sins of humankind, and that His resurrection from the dead guarantees eternal life to all who believe, can be traced back to Paul, not Jesus. Paraphrasing Alfred N. Whitehead's comment that all of Western philosophy "consists of a series of footnotes to Plato," it has often been said that all of Christian theology is a series of footnotes to Paul.

Paul's Life & Writings

According to the Acts of the Apostles, Paul was born in Tarsus, a city in the Roman province of Cilicia, in what is present-day southeast Turkey. He was a deeply religious Jew who was a member of the Pharisees, a strict orthodox Jewish sect. As Paul states himself, he at first persecuted the early followers of Jesus. This ended when he had a mystical experience on the road to Damascus approximately seven years after the crucifixion of Jesus, during which he had a vision of the resurrected Christ. After his conversion, Paul became a missionary to the Gentiles, the non-Jewish followers of Jesus, creating churches in cities and towns throughout Asia Minor and Europe. Despite evidence in Paul's own letters that he was at odds with the apostles in Jerusalem, over the centuries the fissure between Paul and the apostles in Jerusalem was erased in Christian doctrine, and Paul became linked with Peter, the first pope, in history, tradition and art, as one of the two pillars of the church.

There is ongoing dispute among theologians, biblical scholars and historians as to which of Paul's letters are authentic and which were written many years after his death by a number of different authors. Seven of the letters have been accepted universally as written by Paul, three may be authentic, and three are clearly pseudonymous.[17] There is also a question as to the historical validity of some of the events in Paul's life depicted in the Acts of the Apostles, which was written anonymously but traditionally attributed to Luke, and which at times

---

[17] The seven authentic letters are Romans, Galatians, 1 and 2 Corinthians, Philemon, Philippians, and 1 Thessalonians. Three letters—2 Thessalonians, Colossians and Ephesians—are the subject of debate. Scholars agree that 1 and 2 Timothy and Titus were not written by Paul and were likely written as much as a hundred years after his death. James Dunn and John Rogerson, *Eerdmans Commentary on the Bible* (Grand Rapids, MI: Wm. B. Eerdmans Publishing Co., 2003), 1274.

differs from Paul's own letters. However, historically all the Pauline letters, as well as the story of his works in the Acts of the Apostles, were accepted as authentic, considered part of the scriptures, and integrated into the theology and liturgy of the Christian church as it developed.

Paul's Theory of the Soul

As shown above, there are only scattered references to the soul in the four Gospels of the scriptures, and there is no clear theology of the soul or of the resurrection set forth. Instead, the origin of the Christian doctrine on the soul can be found in the epistles written by Paul and those attributed to him by orthodox Christianity. Throughout his letters, Paul makes few references to the historical Jesus or to events in the four Gospels. Rather, he focuses on what was revealed to him in his visions of Christ and bases his theological authority on the revelations he received directly from the resurrected Jesus.

> For I would have you know, brethren, that the gospel which was preached by me is not according to man. For I neither received it from man, nor was I taught it, but I received it through a revelation of Jesus Christ.

Paul asserts that he was chosen by God in his mother's womb to receive the revelations from the risen Jesus and to preach to the Gentiles. He considers himself not in the least inferior to "the most eminent apostles," having "worked harder" than the other apostles. According to Paul, his teaching is more important than that of the original apostles, as he states, "Even though we have known Christ according to the flesh, yet now we know Him in this way no longer."

Pauline theology is based on the divine Jesus Christ, the resurrected Lord, who died for the sins of mankind. Paul teaches that those who believe in and are baptized "in Christ" will themselves be resurrected on the last day. The faith that Paul speaks of is faith in the heavenly Jesus that was revealed to him; in contrast, the faith of the twelve apostles was faith in the words of Jesus given to those who knew Him. And the resurrection that Paul preaches is not based on the gospel story of the empty tomb but on the experience of transformation from mortality to immortality through the spirit of the risen Lord. As we will discuss in chapter five, it is possible to understand Paul's theology of the soul as revealing a teaching of *esoteric Christianity*. The church fathers interpreted these same teachings quite differently, however, and it was those interpretations that became the Roman Catholic Church's theology on the soul and the resurrection.

Paul of Tarsus (Rembrandt)

In his far-reaching treatise *Life after Death*, biblical scholar Alan Segal provides a detailed analysis of Paul's "soul" language. Segal notes that Paul places his focus on the resurrection and never addresses directly the belief of the Greeks in an immortal soul that sheds the body at death, which was predominant at the time. Segal argues that the language Paul uses to describe the soul must be understood as being, in part, a rejection of the Platonic dualism that was prevalent in the Hellenistic Roman society of his day. For, as Segal notes, if the soul is immortal by nature, as Plato claims, and it is the highest form of immortality to be achieved, then the sacrifice of Jesus Christ is unnecessary. Paul skillfully avoids challenging the immortal soul of Plato directly. Instead, describing his own mystical experience, he says,

> Boasting is necessary, though it is not profitable; but I will go on to visions and revelations of the Lord. I know a man in Christ who fourteen years ago— whether in the body I do not know, or out of the body I do not know, God knows— such a man was caught up to the third heaven. And I know how such a man—whether in the body or apart from the body I do not know, God knows—was caught up in Paradise and heard inexpressible words, which a man is not permitted to speak. On behalf of such a man I will boast; but on my own behalf I will not boast.

As Segal points out, Paul does not use the Greek term *psyche* here to effectuate his mystical ascendance, as doing so would have meant he was describing an event in which he left his body behind, evoking the immortal soul of Plato. Instead, Paul states that he does not know whether he is in the body or outside the body during his visionary experience.

While the authors of the Gospels readily use the Greek term *psyche* for the soul in a variety of contexts, Paul creates his own lexicon to describe the soul—that which will be resurrected in Christ. This is what Segal refers to as Paul's pneumatology. Rather than arguing against the Platonic notion of the immortal soul, Paul uses language to emphasize "the notion of spirit to explicate how the physical body of believers would be *transformed* by the Spirit of God." [Emphasis added.]

As Segal explains, in Greek the term *soma physikon* commonly would be used to refer to the physical body; the term *soma sarkikon* would mean specifically the fleshy body. Paul uses neither of these but instead uses the term *soma psychikon*—a combination of the word for soul with the term for body, thus the "ensouled body." This is the totality of the Platonic ensouled body, composed of matter and soul both, and therefore corruptible. Paul contrasts the Platonic ensouled body with the term *soma pneumatikon* (spiritual body) to reference that which is resurrected. What Paul is doing is contrasting the Platonic view of humanity (the unredeemed body composed of soul and flesh) with his own view of the redeemed body, one that has been transformed by the Spirit. The *soma psychikon*—ensouled body—is the ordinary body of flesh and soul; the *soma pneumatikon* is the ordinary body subsumed and transformed by spirit—that is, the resurrected spiritual body that is equivalent to the body of Christ. "And so the new body that God gives his faithful in the resurrection will be a pneumatic or spiritual body."

Thus, Paul creates a new language of the soul that is about resurrected spiritual bodies in the image of the resurrected divine Jesus Christ. In doing so, he also provides a detailed explication of what happens to the souls of believers and of sinners at the final judgment. All this assumes some sort of immortality but focuses on the transformed spiritual body of the believers rather than immortality of all souls, despite the fact that all will either be damned or redeemed.

Paul's vision of the resurrection greatly expands the teaching on the resurrection in the Gospels. In 1 Corinthians 15, often called Paul's resurrection chapter, he states,

> Behold, I tell you a mystery; we will not all sleep, but we will all be changed, in a moment, in the twinkling of an eye, at the last trumpet; for the trumpet will sound, and the dead will be raised imperishable, and we will be changed. For this perishable must put on the imperishable, and this mortal must put on immortality. But when this perishable will have put on the imperishable, and this mortal will have put on immortality, then will come about the saying that is written, "Death is swallowed up in victory."

In 2 Corinthians 5, he describes the body of the *soma pneumatikon* (the ordinary body subsumed and transformed by spirit), "For we know that when this earthly tent we live in is taken down [that is, when we die and leave this earthly body], we will have a house in heaven, an eternal body made for us by God himself and not by human hands. We grow weary in our present bodies, and we long to put on our heavenly bodies like new clothing. For we will put on heavenly bodies; we will not be spirits without bodies."

Until he was close to his own death, Paul always expected that the resurrection he foretold would happen during his lifetime. This resurrection occurs on the final Day of Judgment, the end time or *parousia*, when the eternal fate of each soul will be determined. As he says in Romans,

> But because of your stubbornness and unrepentant heart you are storing up wrath for yourself in the day of wrath and revelation of the righteous judgment of God, who will render to each person according to his deeds: to those who by perseverance in doing good seek for glory and honor and immortality, eternal life; but to those who are selfishly ambitious and do not obey the truth, but obey unrighteousness, wrath and indignation. There will be tribulation and distress for every soul of man who does evil, of the Jew first but also of the Greek, but glory and honor and peace to everyone who does good, to the Jew first and also to the Greek.

This theme is repeated frequently in Paul. For example, he tells the Corinthians, "For we must all appear before the judgment seat of Christ, so that each one may be recompensed for his deeds in the body, according to what he has done, whether good or bad." And in his sixth letter to the Romans, he states, "For the wages of sin is death, but the free gift of God is eternal life in Jesus Christ our Lord."

The resurrected body of Pauline theology is not only eternal but beyond the common distinctions of ordinary life, as Paul tells the Galatians:

> For you are all sons of God through faith in Christ Jesus. For all of you who are baptized into Christ have clothed yourselves with Christ. There is neither Jew nor Greek, there is neither slave nor free, there is neither male nor female; for you are all one in Christ Jesus.

The teaching of Paul, which was adopted by the church, provides a theology of the soul and its resurrection that cannot be found in the Gospels. Based on his own mystical experiences, Paul's teaching goes beyond the gospel stories of the resurrection and Jesus's appearances to the apostles in the flesh to a completely new plane. What the Gospels describe literally, Paul describes in visionary and mystical terms. And it was Paul's version that had the greatest impact on the theology of the soul and resurrection that developed in the Catholic Church, most particularly on the theologians Augustine and Thomas Aquinas.

CHAPTER FOUR

AUGUSTINE & AQUINAS

DEVELOPING THE TRADITIONAL CHRISTIAN THEORY OF THE SOUL

LIVING AND WRITING ALMOST NINE CENTURIES APART, THE CHRISTIAN THEOLOGIANS AUGUSTINE OF HIPPO AND THOMAS AQUINAS nevertheless were each responsible for integrating the teachings of the ancient Greek philosophers with Christian theology in a way that profoundly impacted Christian teaching on the soul. Augustine, relying on Plato's concept of an immaterial soul in a material body, taught that at death, the soul, being immortal, separates from the body, which has merely been its temporary abode. Aquinas, rejecting Augustine's theory that the soul exists separately from the body, relied instead on Aristotle to argue that human beings are a composite of the body and soul, and that the soul, while immortal, does not have a separate existence from the body. Despite their contradictory theories of the soul, both used Paul's teaching on the immaterial spiritual body to construct their bridge connecting Christian theology to ancient Greek philosophy.

Augustine of Hippo

Augustine of Hippo (Antonello da Messina)

His Life & Writings

The teachings of Augustine of Hippo (354–430 CE), considered the greatest of the early Christian philosophers and theologians, merged Paul's theology of the resurrection with the Platonic concept of the soul to give us the immortal soul of Christianity.[18] Many have argued that had it not been for Augustine's fusion of Platonic and Neoplatonic teaching with Christian theology, Plato's works would have been declared heretical by the Roman Catholic Church and lost during the Dark Ages. Augustine's training in classical Greek philosophy strongly influenced his early writings, and his later works were influenced by the writings of Paul. According to eminent religious historian Elaine Pagels,

---

[18] "What is remarkable is the extent to which Augustine was prepared to read back the characteristic teaching of the Christian church into the works of the philosophers, Plato in particular.... in Augustine's treatment of ethical topics the characteristically Christian themes and distinctively Platonic concepts are so closely interwoven that they are often inseparable." R. A. Markus, "St. Augustine," in *Encyclopedia of Philosophy*, ed. Paul Edwards (New York: Macmillan Publishing and The Free Press, 1972), 202.

the importance of Augustine's impact on the development of Christian theology—not only of the soul but also on free will, divine grace, sex, original sin, and predestination—cannot be overstated.

Augustine lived during a crucial point in Western history, in late antiquity, the turning point between the classical period and the Middle Ages, which occurred near the end of the transition from Roman paganism to Christianity. Although the Roman emperor Constantine had converted to Christianity forty years before Augustine was born, there was still furious debate among Christian sects, as well as between Christians and Roman pagans, about many issues, including the question of the soul. Further, the apocalyptic perspective of Paul and the early Christian fathers, who had assumed that the resurrection and Second Coming of Christ would occur during their lifetimes, had proven to be incorrect. Two centuries later, life continued, and the resurrection that Christianity promised to reward the faithful was no longer imminent. As Segal points out, in order to maintain the theological premise that salvation was only attainable through faith in Christ's death and resurrection, there needed to be an interim state—heaven and hell—in which souls were rewarded or punished while waiting for the Second Coming of Christ. This could be achieved through the synthesis of the Christian doctrine of the resurrection of the dead with the Platonic concept of the immortal soul. If all souls lived forever, then sinners could be punished and the faithful rewarded, however long the period of time until the final Day of Judgment. Augustine was primarily responsible for this synthesis.

Augustine was born in 354 CE in Thagaste, a small town in present-day Algeria, to a pagan farmer and a devout Christian mother about whom he wrote extensively and who was later canonized Saint Monica. Despite his modest background, Augustine was a brilliant student of the Greek and Roman classics. At the age of eighteen, Augustine read Cicero's *Hortensius*, which exhorted him to "love and seek and pursue and hold fast and strongly embrace wisdom itself, wherever found." Leaving North Africa for Italy, he became a teacher of literature and rhetoric in Carthage, Rome and Milan. In Carthage, he began a monogamous relationship that lasted over twelve years with a woman of lower social status who bore him a son. For nine years, he was a follower of Manichaeism, an unorthodox Christian sect that taught a rigid dualism between good and evil, spirit and matter, referred to as the

Light and the Darkness. According to its founder, the Mesopotamian Mani, evil existed separately and independently of the divine, coexistent and coeternal, and the soul was a particle of the divine light that was imprisoned in the body of man in darkness. Augustine later wrote numerous encyclicals repudiating the heresy of the Manichees, arguing that the Manichean claim that the soul is a fragmented particle of the Light (i.e., God) made the human soul divine and ignored the distinction between the creator and the created.

During his lifetime, Augustine completed over a hundred voluminous works, some of which were written over long periods of time, as well as more than 200 letters and close to 400 sermons. Many of his writings were intended to directly refute other teachings, including Manichaeism and Pelagianism.[19] His works expounding his theories of the soul include *On the Immortality of the Soul* (386–387 CE), *On the Magnitude of the Soul* (387–388 CE), *On the Two Souls, Against the Manichees* (392–393 CE), *Confessions* (397–401 CE), *On the Origins of the Soul* (419–421 CE), *City of God* (413–427 CE), and *Reconsiderations* (426–427 CE). His *Sermon 362* (410 CE) also provides an extensive treatment of the soul in the context of the resurrection. Two of Augustine's works, *Confessions* and *City of God*, are considered masterpieces and classics of Western literature.

In *Confessions*, Augustine's autobiography, he describes the years he spent teaching in Milan, during which he studied the Neoplatonists, particularly Plotinus and Porphyry, under the tutelage of Ambrose, the bishop of Milan.[20] Augustine speaks at length of the impact of these

---

[19] The Pelagian controversy involved a fierce philosophical and theological debate over the nature of original sin and the role of divine grace in overcoming it. The Pelagians denied the doctrine of original sin, believing that free will gave all human beings the ability to make moral choices and that divine grace was an aid to living a moral, sinless Christian life. In contrast, near the end of his life, Augustine argued that original sin is "universally debilitating and insuperable without the aid of unmerited grace, and that God has predestined only a small number of people to be saved." Mendelson, 18 (quoting Augustine in *City of God*, XXI.12).

[20] Augustine's *Confessions* tells the story of the first thirty-five years of his life. In it can be found his famous quote, "Lord, grant me chastity and continence, but not yet." Augustine, *Confessions*, 145 (VIII.vii.17).

Neoplatonist works—what he refers to as "the books of the Platonists." It was in Milan that Augustine ended his relationship with his mistress, planning to marry a woman of higher social class to further his secular career. But as described in *Confessions*, after reading the epistles of Paul in a Milanese garden, he was instantaneously converted to Christianity and renounced both his future marriage and his career. Augustine was baptized into Christianity by Ambrose in 387 CE. Ordained a priest in 391, he was made a bishop of Hippo in 395.

Augustine's Theory of the Soul

Although Augustine's views on the *origins* of the soul changed significantly during his life, it was axiomatic for him that the *nature* of the human soul is both immortal (from the Neoplatonists) and immaterial (from Paul). That is, a human being is composed of a material body that dies and an immaterial body that is immortal—a "rational soul using a mortal and material body." For Augustine, the death of the human being is the separation of the soul from the body; while the body perishes and dissolves into the elements, the soul is immortal. In *Confessions*, Augustine speaks of the immortality of the soul, stating, for example, "After death the life of the soul remains with the consequence of our acts," and "The deity would not have done all that for us [spread Christianity throughout the world] if with the body's death the soul's life were also destroyed." Likewise, in *Soliloquies* and *On the Immortality of the Soul*, Augustine also makes arguments derived from Plato and the Neoplatonists, positing the following:

1. Truth so exists in the soul that it is inseparable from it, and since Truth is immortal, therefore, the soul is immortal.
2. The soul of man is immortal because it is the seat of Reason, which is immortal.
3. The soul is life, and in contrast the body is merely something animated by it; since the soul cannot suffer death because life belongs to its very essence, the soul is immortal.

As Augustine became more deeply involved in the management of the church in his role as a bishop, he made a detailed study of the writings of Paul. "With avid intensity I seized the sacred writings of your Spirit and especially the apostle Paul . . . I began reading and found that all the truth I had read in the Platonists was stated here together with the commendation of your grace. . . . " Augustine went on to state that what was missing in the Platonist books was found in Paul: "'Who will deliver him from this body of death' except this grace through Jesus Christ our Lord."

Augustine relied on Paul to support his emphasis on the immateriality of the soul, synthesizing Paul's concept of the immaterial body (*soma pneumatikon*) with the Platonic concept of the immortal soul. In *Sermon 362*, Augustine states:

> [The heavenly body] will be called a body and it can be called a celestial body. The same thing is said by the Apostle when he distinguishes between bodies: "All flesh is not the same flesh: but one is the flesh of men, another of beasts, another of birds, another of fishes. And there are bodies celestial and bodies terrestrial. (I Cor. 15:39-40). However, he certainly would not say celestial flesh; although bodies may be said to be flesh but only earthly bodies. For all flesh is body; but not every body is flesh. (*Serm.* 362.18.21)

As Segal explains, "Augustine believed that saved Christians would enjoy eternity as a community of perfected beings, like angels." He notes that Augustine would have had a much harder time demonstrating how body and soul go together (i.e., synthesizing the Greeks with Christian teaching) without Paul's notion of the spiritual body.

In *The City of God*, Augustine provides his most extensive treatment of the fate of the soul at the resurrection on the final Day of Judgment. Written over a period of fourteen years after the sack of Rome by the Visigoths in 410 CE, the twenty-two volumes were, in part, a response to the allegations of pagan Romans that the fall of Rome was caused by Christianity. The decline of Rome contradicted not only the Romans' belief, held since the time of Virgil, that the Roman Empire was eternal, but also the more recent Christian belief that Rome was an essential instrument in the divine purpose of history. Augustine used this period in history as a backdrop for his description of the ultimate fate of humanity and the inevitability of divine justice.

Central to an understanding of Augustine's theory of the resurrection in *City of God* is his teaching on original sin. As Elaine Pagels notes, in his earlier writings Augustine follows three centuries of Christian tradition regarding the concept of free will, human freedom and self-government (i.e., the use of free will to make moral choices). But Pagels points out that in *City of God*, "the desire to master one's will, rather than expressing the true nature of rational beings, becomes for Augustine the great and fatal temptation: 'The fruit of the tree of knowledge of good and evil is personal control over one's own will.'" Augustine makes it clear that "the whole human race inherited from Adam a nature irreversibly damaged by sin . . . That semen itself, already 'shackled by the bond of death,' transmits the damage incurred by sin." Pagels comments that for Augustine,

> What epitomizes our rebellion against God, above all, is the "rebellion in the flesh"—a spontaneous uprising, so to speak, in the "disobedient members": "After Adam and Eve disobeyed . . . they felt for the first time a movement of disobedience in their flesh, as punishment in kind for their own disobedience to God. The soul, which had taken a perverse delight in its own liberty and disdained to serve God, was now deprived of its original mastery over the body." [*City of God*, 13, 13] Specifically, Augustine concludes, "the sexual desire (*libido*) of our disobedient members arose in those first human beings as a result of the sin of disobedience . . . and because a shameless movement (*impudens motus*) resisted the rule of their will, they covered their shameful members." [*City of God*, 13, 24] . . . [S]pontaneous sexual desire is, Augustine contends, the clearest evidence of original sin.

Augustine believes that by "defining spontaneous sexual desire as the proof and penalty of original sin he has succeeded in implicating the whole human race, except, of course, for Christ." [21] This radical view of original sin, that action of the human will can have no effect on the

---

[21] "Christ alone of all humankind, Augustine explains, was born without *libido*—being born, he believes, without the intervention of semen that transmits its effect." Pagels, *Adam, Eve, and the Serpent*, 112.

sinful state of the soul, makes original sin irreversible. Humankind has wholly lost its capacity for self-government. Since Christians cannot be trusted to govern themselves by exercising will to make moral choices, Augustine extends this concept to justify endorsing, for the church as well as the state, the whole arsenal of secular government—commands, threats, coercion, penalties, and even physical force. Pagels argues that this justification of the marriage of the church with imperial power explains why Augustine's radical theology, ardently debated for a century after his death, triumphed over earlier Christian understanding of free will. The earlier teachings were eventually declared to be heresy.

Given Augustine's belief in the irredeemable nature of original sin, it is not surprising that he sees the ultimate fate of the souls of most human beings as one of eternal damnation. In the *City of God*, Augustine's view of the resurrection at the end of time, the final Day of Judgment, can be summarized as follows:

> Due to the universal contagion of original sin wherein all have sinned in Adam, humanity has become a mass of the deservedly damned. By means of an utterly unmerited grace, God has chosen a small minority of this mass—the smallness of the number is itself a means whereby God makes apparent what all in fact deserve—and thus human history is composed of the progress of two cities, the city of God and the city of Man: those who by means of grace renounced the self and turn towards God, as opposed to the vast majority who have renounced God and turned towards the self . . . [T]he linear movement of human history aims at the eventual separation of the two cities, in which the members of each city are united with their resurrected bodies and given their respective just rewards: for the small minority saved by unmerited grace, there is the vision of God, a joy we can only dimly discern at the moment. For the overwhelming mass of humanity, there is the second death wherein their resurrected bodies will be subject to eternal torment by flames that will inflict pain without consuming the body, the degree of torment proportional to the extent of sin, although the duration is equal in all cases: they must suffer without end, for to suffer any less would

be to contradict scripture and undermine our confidence in
the eternal blessedness of the small number God has saved.

Augustine clearly believes that "the disembodied soul experiences the beatitude of heaven or the torment of hell. Nevertheless, he also firmly believes in the resurrection of the flesh." How else could the damned be "subject to eternal torment by flames"? Augustine states that at the end of time the resurrected body will be composed of the numerically identical elements out of which the earthly body was composed. In response to objections concerning the possibility of regaining all the elements once the body has decomposed, Augustine argues that an omnipotent god can bring them back together. Likewise, he posits that just because human experience cannot conceive of a body lasting forever in a burning fire, it does not mean that this is impossible with the power of the Almighty. For Augustine states,

> Although it be true that in this world there is no flesh which can suffer pain and yet cannot die, yet in the world to come there shall be flesh such as now there is not, as there will also be death such as now there is not. For death will not be abolished, but will be eternal, since the soul will neither be able to enjoy God and live, nor to die and escape the pains of the body. *The first death drives the soul from the body against her will; the second death holds the soul in the body against her will.* The two have this in common, that the soul suffers against her will what her own body inflicts. [Emphasis added.]

In contrast to the fate of most of humankind, the souls of those who will be saved by unmerited grace will have an incorruptible body for their reward. For them, Augustine sees a resurrected spiritual body that is "both infinitely superior to the soul and, at the same time, only complete when it has become a spiritual body. Augustine analogizes with incarnation: If God can incarnate, then the perfected soul can be embodied as a spiritual body."

While confident about the fate of souls on the final Day of Judgment, Augustine was unable to reach a conclusion as to the *origins* of the soul. During his lifetime, Augustine developed five distinct theories of the origin of man's soul. His first two theories, strongly influenced by Plato, were set forth in *On the Immortality of the Soul* (387 CE) and *On the Magnitude of the Soul* (387–88 CE). All five theories assumed the soul's existence prior to embodiment—that is, Augustine alternatively hypothesizes:

1. The soul is sent by God to direct the body.
2. The soul, by its own choice, comes to inhabit the body.
3. This second theory would evolve to include the notion of sin and the idea that the soul was subject to reincarnation in Augustine's *Letter 166*.
4. All souls beginning from Adam were passed from parent to child.
5. God created a new soul for each body.

Later in life, in *On the Soul and its Origins* (419 CE) and elsewhere, Augustine spoke only of the last two theories, rejecting the earlier theories as violating Christian theology. He also suggested a new theory, found in *City of God* and elsewhere, that God created only one soul—the soul of Adam—and that all later souls were not mere offspring of Adam's soul but identical to Adam's soul prior to embodiment. This theory supported Augustine's theory of original sin, as well as his belief in the damnation of the souls of unbaptized infants. Near the end of his life, Augustine wrote *Retractations* (426–427 CE) (English: *Reconsiderations*), a book in which he revisited his previous works and spoke unfavorably of some of his early theories on the soul. Despite pressure from his contemporaries, however, at the end of his life, Augustine was unwilling to take a decisive stand on the origin of the soul, referring to the question as obscure and difficult.

Thomas Aquinas

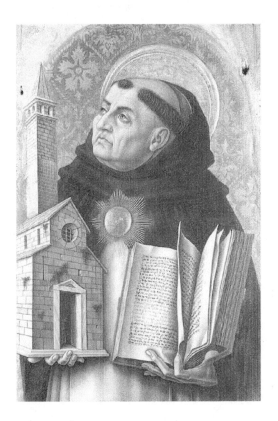

Thomas Aquinas (Carlo Crivelli)

His Life & Writings

Just as Augustine was responsible for incorporating Platonism into Christian theology, Thomas Aquinas (1225–1274), the most renowned of medieval theologians, reworked Aristotle to comport with Christian theology. It has frequently been said that Aquinas "baptized" Aristotle. Historian David Knowles has argued that Aquinas, who became known as the Angelic Doctor of the Church, created a completely new and original Christian philosophy that rejected the Augustinian-Platonist view of the soul. Like Augustine, Aquinas relied on the epistles of Paul, in particular on Paul's teachings of the resurrection of the spiritual body in 1 Corinthians 15, to provide the biblical authority that supported Aquinas's new, and some asserted, heretical Aristotelian teaching on the soul. While controversial in his own time and for the half century following his death, the teachings of Aquinas later became known as Thomism, and in 1879, Pope Leo XIII issued the encyclical *Aeterni Patris*, in which he exhorted Catholic institutions to "restore the golden wisdom of St. Thomas, and to spread it far and wide for the defense and beauty of the Catholic faith, for the good of society, and for the advantage of all the sciences."

Thomas Aquinas lived during the period known as the High Middle Ages, eight centuries after Augustine's death. During Aquinas's lifetime, the Roman Catholic Church, which had broken from the Eastern Orthodox Church in 1054, exercised unprecedented power over the feudal kings who ruled the various parts of Europe. Popes were not only heads of the church but they were also secular princes. Although Aquinas considered himself a simple Dominican friar, he was comfortable in the company of popes and spent long periods of his life in the great medieval universities of Europe. During his forty-nine years, Aquinas wrote over sixty volumes, including commentaries on nearly the entire corpus of Aristotle, as well as five volumes on the epistles of Paul. Other important works include *On Being and Essence* (1252–1256), *On the Principles of Nature* (1252–1259), *On the Eternity of the World* (1256–1271), and *On There Being Only One Intellect* (1270). In his most famous work, *Summa Theologica* (1264–1273), which he intended as a compendium of Roman Catholic doctrine for beginning theology students, Aquinas set forth in detail his theory of the soul and its origins.

Aquinas was born in 1225 into an aristocratic Italian family at Roccasecca, a hilltop castle midway between Rome and Naples, during the period of the great duel between the popes and the German emperors who called themselves the Holy Roman Emperors. Frederick II, the Holy Roman Emperor, was his cousin. Thomas was the youngest son of eleven children, with little prospect of significant inheritance of title, money or property. When he was only five years old, he was sent to the Benedictine monks at the abbey of Monte Cassino, where he spent ten years as an oblate (not ordained as a monk), learning to read and write and living under the Benedictine rule. At the age of fourteen, he was sent to the newly founded University of Naples, where he lived in the Benedictine house and studied natural philosophy, which meant Aristotle, until he finished his baccalaureate studies.

Then, in April of 1244, Thomas shocked his family by joining the Dominicans, a new order of mendicant monks who took a vow of poverty and lived as itinerant preachers. Appalled, his mother sent two of his brothers to kidnap him; they imprisoned him in the family castle at Roccasecca for over a year. Legend has it that in an attempt to dissuade him from a Dominican future, his brothers sent a beautiful prostitute into his room. As the story is told,

> Thomas snatched a brand from the fire and drove the poor girl from the room. Then, with the charred end of the stick, he traced a cross on the wall and fell on his knees before it . . . An angel is said to have appeared before him and tied a cincture around his waist, and from that time Thomas was untroubled by carnal temptation. This as much as his subsequent theology is the origin of his title as the angelic doctor.

Aquinas, now accepted by his family as a Dominican friar, went on to study in the great universities in Paris and Cologne, obtaining a master of arts at the age of twenty. In Cologne, he was so quiet that he was nicknamed "The Dumb Ox," having been described as "a huge bull of a man, fat and slow and quiet; very mild and magnanimous but not very social; shy, even apart from the humility of holiness; and abstracted, even apart from his occasional and carefully concealed experiences of trance or ecstasy." From there, Aquinas returned to Paris where he began his official training in theology, a long and grueling course of study to become a master of sacred theology. Throughout the rest of his life, he taught and wrote both in Paris and in various places throughout Italy, becoming a key figure in the medieval school known as Scholasticism. Aquinas's masterpiece, *Summa Theologica*, eventually came to be considered the pinnacle of Scholastic, medieval, and Christian philosophy.

Aquinas's Theory of the Soul

Within the 3,500 pages of his masterpiece, Aquinas relied on Aristotle, whom he referred to simply as "the Philosopher," to develop a doctrine of the soul. Aquinas's doctrine focused on the concept of the animating force, which he described as "the first principle of life of those things that live." According to Aquinas (and Aristotle), the soul does not exist separately from the body, merely making temporary use of it, as the Augustinian Platonists believed and the church had accepted for centuries; instead, the soul actually takes the form of the body, it is "the substantial form of the body," and a human being is a composite of body and soul. The body is the primary matter and the soul the substantial form of man. For Aquinas, the soul is immaterial—that is, spiritual and immortal—and its union with the body is essential to the soul and characteristic of its nature. In other words, there cannot be an existent soul that is not the soul *of* some body, and it is the soul that animates the human body. The scholar Denys Turner put it this way in describing Aquinas,

> Emphatically he denies that I am my soul—the "I" that I am does not consist in the soul that I have, and a bodiless person is no person. So emphatic is Thomas in insisting that no human person can exist without a body that you may well find yourself asking why he needs to speak of the soul at all, since all he seems to mean by "soul" is whatever it is that accounts for a body's being alive.

Like Aristotle, Aquinas rejected the Platonic concept of three distinct souls or forms, a "vegetative soul" with the functions of nutrition, growth, and reproduction; an "animal soul" capable of sense perception; and a "rational soul," the intellect or mind, each accounting for some part of what it means to be human. For Aquinas, this would destroy the unity of the person. Instead, he asserts that in man, the vegetative, sensitive and intellectual souls are numerically one. Human beings have one soul, an "intellectual" soul, which is wholly vegetative, wholly animal, and wholly rational in nature. Aquinas's theory of the soul was controversial not because he denied that human beings have a soul (which he did not) nor for asserting that human beings have an "intellectual" soul, which his Augustinian Platonist critics also believed—he was criticized and his teaching deemed heretical for stating that human beings have only *one* soul, which does not have a separate existence from the body.

As Denys Turner points out, a dilemma arises for Aquinas in the apparent contradiction between his assertion "that I am not my soul, that my soul is my body's form, its source of life, and that if *only* my soul were to survive death I would not . . ." [emphasis added], and his belief in personal immortality—that is, the core Christian doctrine of the resurrection of the body, the immortality of the individual, which he does not dispute.[22] For if the soul is the form of the body, how can it survive the death of the body?

It is in Paul that Aquinas finds the solution to these seemingly mutually exclusive propositions. As Aquinas says, "It would not be easy, indeed it would be difficult, to sustain the immortality of the soul without the resurrection of the body." The soul cannot die, Aquinas says, relying on Aristotle, because "the human soul, which is called the intellect or the mind, is something incorporeal and subsistent." These "intellectual" powers of the soul, Aquinas says in his *Commentaries on the Epistles of St. Paul,* are "spiritual." Aquinas points to 1 Corinthians 15, analyzing Paul's statement, "It is sown a physical body, it is raised a spiritual body," and states,

> One should also consider that there is a threefold difference in the powers of the soul. For some powers are such that their activities are directed to the good of the body, i.e. the generative, nutritive and augmentative; some there are that use bodily organs, as the power of the sensitive part, but their activity is not directly ordained to the body, but rather to the perfection of the soul. But there are some powers which neither use bodily organs nor are directly ordained to the good of the body, but more to the good of the soul, as those which pertain to the intellective part.

---

[22] "This doctrine that the soul survives the body and is immortal, that is, it cannot naturally die, was a doctrine of much Greek philosophy universally defended in Thomas' time and before, although its official proclamation as Catholic teaching awaited a decree of the Fifth Lateran Council in 1515, centuries after Thomas' death." Turner, 74–76.

Aquinas goes on to state, "In the resurrected state the animal (physical) activities of the body will cease, because there will be no generation, no growth or nourishment, but the body without any impediment and weariness will unceasingly serve the soul in its spiritual activities . . . Therefore, just as our body is now animal (physical), then it will be truly *spiritual*." [Emphasis added.] Challenging the Platonists, Aquinas says, "Some have interpreted this badly and said that in the resurrection the body is changed into a spirit and will be similar to air or the wind, which is called a spirit . . . the Apostle does not say that a spirit will rise, but a *spiritual* body. Therefore, in the resurrection it will be *spiritual*, not a spirit, just as now it is animal, not soul." [Emphasis added.]

For Aquinas, the soul is immortal not because it exists separately from the physical body. The soul is naturally immortal, capable of existing independently of the earthly body, because it is "intellectual"—that is, it is immaterial—and being immaterial, it is not subject to the natural corruption of the body. It is the spiritual nature of the *resurrected* body, as set forth in Paul, that Aquinas relies on to establish the immortality of the unified "intellectual soul," which cannot exist without some sort of body.

Thus, while Aquinas disputed the Augustinian concept of the soul, he agreed with Augustine's theory of the resurrection of the body.[23] Analyzing Paul's statement in 1 Corinthians 15 that "flesh and blood cannot inherit the kingdom of God," Aquinas states,

> What we must not think, as some heretics say, is that flesh and blood will not rise according to substance, but rather that the whole body will be changed into spirit or air. This is heretical and false. For the Apostle says that our body will be conformed to his body of radiance. Therefore, since Christ

---

[23] Aquinas also accepted in large part the Augustinian concept of original sin, focusing on its impact on the nature of the soul rather than its impact on the power of the soul, i.e., the will. Aquinas, *Summa Theologica* Ia IIae.83.2. Aquinas rejected the Augustinian belief that human beings had no free will, but contended that a person could act virtuously, even without the assistance of grace, stating, "Grace does not dispense with nature; it perfects it." *Summa Theologica*, I.8.2.

after his resurrection, has body and blood, . . . it is certain that we too will have flesh and blood in the resurrection.

Addressing the apparent contradiction, Aquinas explains that by "flesh and blood," Paul does not mean that the substance of flesh and blood cannot inherit the kingdom of God, "but rather flesh and blood, i.e., those devoting themselves to flesh and blood, namely, men given to vices and lust, cannot inherit the kingdom of God." And he notes, "after the resurrection the body will not be subject to the corruption of the flesh and blood, as it is of the man who lives now." As to the personal nature of immortality, Aquinas states that what remains in the soul after the destruction of the body are the powers of intelligence and will. "For the soul, even after separation from the body, retains the being which accrued to it while in the body."

Regarding the *origins* of the soul, Aquinas took the view that God created each new soul from nothing and participated in the human act of procreation by endowing the embryo with a sensitive soul and, later, a rational soul. This explains why Aquinas put such emphasis on the sanctity of human reproduction and claimed that the begetting and raising of children was the primary purpose of married life. Aquinas also rejected any suggestion that the soul is of the "divine substance."

During his lifetime, Aquinas's theory of the soul was challenged by two sets of opponents, the Christian Augustinian Platonists, primarily Franciscans, and the Latin Averroists, primarily Islamic scholars who adopted twelfth-century Muslim philosopher Averroes's interpretations of Aristotle's theories on the nature of the soul. The two groups actually agreed with one another in their dispute with Aquinas. They both followed Plato, separating the soul from the body, rejecting Aquinas's unification of the soul and the body. However, their reliance on Plato was in support of different theories. For the Averroists, there was only one single intellectual soul, a piece of which is in each individual human being; and for the Platonist Augustinians, there was an individuated intellectual soul separated from the animal and vegetative life of a person.

In the midst of this heated controversy, Aquinas stopped writing. His secretary, Friar Reginald of Piperno, tells the story of a mystical experience that occurred to Aquinas on Saint Nicholas Day, December 6, 1273. Thereafter, when asked to complete the *Summa Theologica* and respond to this controversy, Aquinas reportedly said to Reginald, "I can write no more. I have seen things which make all my writings like straw."

Three months later, on his way to the Council of Lyon, Aquinas fell ill. He died on March 7, 1274, at the Cistercian abbey at Fossanova. In 1277, three years after his death, a commission established by the bishop of Paris condemned as heretical 219 propositions, many of them Aquinas's tenets, and banned them from being taught. During the fifty years following his death, Aquinas's works were highly controversial, but eventually the ban was lifted. Aquinas was canonized a saint in 1323, and in 1567, he was proclaimed a Doctor of the Church.

As can be seen, despite the distinctions that Aquinas took great pains to draw between his theology of the soul and that of Augustine, the reality is that they stand as the two pillars of Christian theology prior to the modern period, differing primarily in their views on the *nature* of the soul and its relation to the body. Both Augustine and Aquinas relied on the language of Paul, rather than the language of the Synoptic Gospels, to support their conceptualizations of the immortality of the soul. For both, Paul's language of the spiritual body in 1 Corinthians 15 was proof of the resurrection of all human beings at the end of time, when each immortal soul would be rewarded or punished eternally. However, as we will see in the next chapter, Paul's language regarding the spiritual body can be interpreted quite differently, in a way that illuminates strong parallels to The Fourth Way teaching of Gurdjieff on the soul.

CHAPTER FIVE

ESOTERIC CHRISTIANITY & THE FOURTH WAY

The Fourth Way & the Origins of Esoteric Christianity

G. I. GURDJIEFF TELLS US THAT EACH GENUINE RELIGION HAS TWO PARTS, THE *EXOTERIC* AND THE *ESOTERIC*.

> Every real religion, that is, one that has been created by learned people for a definite aim, consists of two parts. One part [*exoteric*] teaches *what* is to be done. This part becomes common knowledge and in the course of time is distorted and departs from the original. The other part [*esoteric*] teaches *how* to do what the first part teaches. This part is preserved in secret in special schools and with its help it is always possible to rectify what has been distorted in the first part or to restore what has been forgotten. . . . This secret part exists in Christianity also as well as in other religions and it teaches *how* to carry out the precepts of Christ and what they really mean.

Gurdjieff speaks of Christ as one of several Messengers from Above, describing Jesus as a saint but also speaking of Saint Buddha, Saint Mohammed, Saint Lama, and Saint Moses. He tells us, "All the great genuine religions which have existed down to the present time . . . are always based on the same truths." These truths, however, are by "the first generation" of followers so distorted that the information that "reached the beings of subsequent generations [was] suitable perhaps only for the inventing of what are called 'children's fairy tales.'" Regarding Christianity, he says that early in its development, what became the orthodox teaching of the church was mixed with Judaism, which had by that time "already been thoroughly distorted." During the Middle Ages, Christianity was further distorted by the "fantastic doctrine" of hell and heaven imported from Babylonian dualism by the church fathers. For a variety of political and other reasons, Gurdjieff notes, the fathers of the church mixed fragments from other religious teachings, which "had not only nothing in common with the teaching of Jesus, but which sometimes even flatly contradicted the truths this Divine Teacher taught." Think of what it took, Gurdjieff points out, "to come from the Gospel preaching of love to the Inquisition; or to go from the ascetics of the early centuries studying *esoteric* Christianity to the scholastics who calculated how many angels could be placed on the point of a needle." Using humor to emphasize his point, Gurdjieff says,

> If the followers of this great religion themselves, especially those who are called the "elders of the church" of the Middle Ages, treated this religion, step by step, as "Bluebeard" treated his wives, that is to say, put them in derision and changed all their beauty and charms, that is already quite a different matter.

Like all *exoteric* religions, Gurdjieff tells us, the numerous forms of Christianity that developed from the orthodox Christian teachings are of three types. The first is "a religion that consists of rites, of external forms, of sacrifices and ceremonies of imposing splendor and brilliance, or, on the contrary, of a gloomy, cruel, and savage character, and so on." The second is a religion "of faith, love, adoration, impulse, enthusiasm, which soon becomes transformed into the religion of persecution, oppression, and extermination of 'heretics' and 'heathens.'" The third is an "intellectual, theoretical religion of proofs and arguments, based upon logical deductions, consideration and interpretations." He goes on to say that, "Religions number one, number two, and number three are really the only ones we know; all known and existing religions and denominations in the world belong to one of these three categories."

Regarding Christianity specifically, Gurdjieff said, "there exists a Christianity number one, that is to say, paganism [idol worship] in the guise of Christianity. Christianity number two is an emotional religion, sometimes very pure but without force, sometimes full of bloodshed and horror leading to the Inquisition, to religious wars. Christianity number three, instances of which are afforded by various forms of Protestantism, is based upon dialectic, argument, theories, and so forth. Then there is Christianity number four, of which men number one, number two, and number three have no conception whatever."[24]

Gurdjieff tells us that the aim of all *esoteric* religions is to teach the way to immortality; that is, while human beings are not born with an immortal soul, as images of God we possess a seed from which it is possible to develop one.

> All [esoteric] religious teachings strive to show the way to it. There are a great many ways, some shorter and some longer, some harder and some easier, but all, without exception, lead or strive to lead in one direction, that is, to immortality. [25]

When asked about his teaching of The Fourth Way and its relationship to contemporary Christianity, Gurdjieff replied, *"this is esoteric Christianity."*

Gurdjieff makes it clear that the origins of *esoteric* Christianity come from prehistoric Egypt: "It will seem strange to many people when I say that this prehistoric Egypt was Christian many thousands of years before the birth of Christ, that is to say, that its religion was composed

---

[24] Patterson points out that the first three religions are subjective and correspond to people who are primarily "instinctual [man number one], emotional [man number two] or intellectual [man number three]." Patterson, "Gurdjieff & Christianity," in *Georgi Ivanovitch Gurdjieff*, 520.

[25] Traditionally, there were three ways: (1) the way of the fakir (the physical body), (2) the way of the monk (faith and religious feeling), and (3) the way of the yogi (knowledge and the mind). *Search*, 44. The Fourth Way works on all three simultaneously; there is no faith involved. Instead, the fundamental principle is the demand for understanding. *Search*, 49.

of the same principles and ideas that constitute true Christianity." He explained,

> The Christian church, the Christian form of worship was not invented by the fathers of the church. It was all taken in a ready-made form from Egypt, only not from the Egypt that we know but from one which we do not know. This Egypt was in the same place as the other but it existed much earlier. Only small bits of it survived in historical times, and these bits have been preserved in secret and so well that we do not even know where they have been preserved.

In an essay, Patterson clarifies that Gurdjieff meant the teaching of ancient Egypt *passed through* Christianity, for the church fathers did not understand it and were confused about its origins.

Astonishingly, Augustine acknowledged near the end of his life that he knew that the Christian religion existed before Christ. In his work *Reconsiderations*, Augustine clarified a prior statement and said,

> For what is now called the Christian religion existed of old and was never absent from the beginning of the human race until Christ came in the flesh. Then true religion which already existed, began to be called Christian. After the resurrection and ascension of Christ into heaven, the apostles began to preach him and many believed, and the disciples were first called Christians in Antioch, as it is written. When I said, "This is the Christian religion in our times," I did not mean that it had not existed in former times, but that it received that name later.

Gurdjieff's statement that The Fourth Way "*is esoteric Christianity*" has profound implications. It places The Fourth Way at the origin of what eventually became Christianity as we know it today—that is, *exoteric* Christianity—as well as the secret *esoteric* Christianity of which Gurdjieff (and Augustine) speak. This *esoteric* Christianity was followed by early Christian sects that understood the secret meaning of Jesus's teachings. During the two centuries immediately following Christ's death, these sects challenged and disputed what became orthodox

Christian teaching. Some of these groups called themselves Gnostics, from the Greek word *gnosis*, meaning knowledge.[26] The Gnostics revered and considered sacred a variety of gospels written by disciples of Jesus and others that were not included in the scriptures, but instead were declared to be heretical by those who selected the orthodox canon. Some of the Gnostic sects, in particular the followers of Valentinus, also relied on the secret *esoteric* teachings of Paul.

When we explore the relationship between Gurdjieff's teaching of the soul and what we know about esoteric Christianity during the centuries immediately following the death of the historical Jesus, we see remarkable similarities. Although many of the teachings of Paul and the Gnostics, at least as we understand them today, do not coincide with the teaching of The Fourth Way, there are significant parallel threads in each. These reveal connections with esoteric Christianity, particularly the teaching that human beings are not born with an immortal soul. We are attempting here to piece together a large puzzle with only a few of the puzzle pieces available to us. Still, it is worthwhile to examine the esoteric teachings in the Gnostic Gospels and in Paul's writings that establish connections to The Fourth Way teachings on the soul.

Esoteric Christianity in the Gnostic Gospels

Prior to the discovery of previously unknown Gnostic texts near Nag Hammadi by Egyptian peasants in 1945, most of what was known

---

[26] There is a debate among scholars about the origins and definition of Gnosticism. "The difficulties in pinning down a definition of Gnosticism are intimately connected with the controversy about its origins. Was it indeed no more than a heretical offshoot, an eccentric and aberrant branch of Christianity, or was it the latest expression of a long, mostly hidden tradition that had existed for centuries before the Christian era?" Stephen Hoeller, *What Is a Gnostic?* The Gnostic Archive, http://gnosis. org/whatisgnostic. htm. Some scholars believe its origin is pre-Christian with Jewish roots, others that it stems from the ancient Iranian religion Zoroastrianism, and others believe it originated in the first century of the Christian era and denotes a heterodox segment of the new Christian community. Elaine Pagels, *The Gnostic Gospels* (New York: Vintage Books, 1979), xxx–xxxiii.

about Gnostic teachings came from anti-Gnostic writings of early church fathers, such as Irenaeus and Tertullian, who declared that Gnosticism was heresy and did all that they could to destroy its traces. However, the discovery in 1945 of the thirteen codices of the Nag Hammadi, with its fifty-two texts—forty of which were previously unknown—revealed a trove of lost scriptures. These included gospels that appear to be written by some of the apostles of Jesus, including the *Gospel of Thomas*, the *Gospel of Phillip*, the *Gospel of Peter*, and the *Apocryphon of James* (Secret Book of James), as well as the *Gospel of Mary Magdalene* and others. Then in 2001, the *Gospel of Judas* was rediscovered, revealing an entirely different story of the role Judas Iscariot played in the crucifixion and death of Jesus from that in the New Testament, one which, as will be discussed below, Gurdjieff wrote about in his book *All and Everything*, published in 1950.

Gnostic themes stood diametrically opposed to the teachings that eventually triumphed in the theological wars of the second and third centuries. As Elaine Pagels notes, the Gnostics challenged the orthodox priests and bishops claiming authority as Peter's successors, arguing that "the orthodox relied solely on the *exoteric* teaching which Christ and the apostles offered to 'the many,' while Gnostic Christians offered, in addition, their *secret teaching*, known only to a few." [Emphasis added.] Marvin Meyer, one of the translators of the *Gospel of Judas* into English, points out that in contrast to the scriptures, in the Gnostic gospels Jesus is primarily a teacher and revealer of wisdom and knowledge, not a savior who dies for the sins of the world. "For gnostics, the fundamental problem in human life is not sin but ignorance, and the best way to address this is not through faith but through knowledge."

While a study of the numerous Gnostic works now available reveals that there was never one single Gnosticism, there clearly exists a broad current of interrelated themes among these teachings. The Gnostics proclaimed that salvation (immortality) is possible only through a revealed secret *gnosis*. This *gnosis* provides a profound awakening that came with the understanding that something within was "uncreated" that must be born. Fundamental to all is that the Gnostic teachings are secret *esoteric* revelations of the divine mysteries reserved only for an elite. For example, the *Gospel of Thomas*, which contains 114 sayings of Jesus introduced by the words "Jesus said," is explicitly a collection of secret sayings communicating secret wisdom:

These are the secret sayings that the living Jesus spoke and Judas Thomas [not Judas Iscariot] the twin recorded. He said, "Whoever finds the interpretation of these sayings will not taste death."

Gospel of Thomas and *The Secret Book of John* (Apocryphon of John), Codex II The Nag Hammadi manuscripts

Alan Segal describes the sayings in the *Gospel of Thomas* as "genuinely puzzling, their purpose apparently to demarcate those with knowledge (*gnosis*) from those without." Elaine Pagels compares them to Zen koans, riddles intended to bring the student to greater understanding of hidden truths.

The *Secret Book of James* begins with a similar statement of the secret nature of the work:

> Since you asked me to send you a secret book revealed to me and Peter by the Lord, I could not turn you down or refuse you. So I have written it in Hebrew, and sent it to you and only you. But, considering that you are a minister for the salvation of the saints, try to be careful not to communicate this book to many people, for the Savior did not even want to communicate it to all of us, his twelve disciples. Nonetheless, blessed are those who will be saved through the faith of this treatise.

And the introduction to the *Gospel of Judas* describes it as, "The secret account of the revelation that Jesus spoke in conversation with Judas Iscariot during a week three days before he celebrated Passover."[27]

Another common thread running through the Gnostic Gospels is the "conviction that direct, personal and absolute knowledge of the authentic truths of existence is accessible to human beings, and, moreover, that the attainment of such knowledge must always constitute the supreme achievement of human life." The Gnostics also shared a belief in the "'uncreated self' the divine seed, the pearl, the spark of knowing: consciousness, intelligence, light." According to the second-century Gnostic Theodotus, *gnosis* is the knowledge of "who we were and what we have become, where we were and into what we have been thrown, wither we hasten and from what we are redeemed, what is birth and what rebirth." Biblical scholar Bart Ehrman describes this key Gnostic belief in more modern language:

---

[27] When Jesus reveals the secrets of the universe to Judas, he tells him, "[Come], that I may teach you about [secrets] no person [has] ever seen. For there exists a great and boundless realm, whose extent no generation of angels has seen, [in which] there is a great invisible [Spirit], which no eye of an angel has ever seen, no thought of the heart has ever comprehended, and it was never called by any name." As Meyer notes, this language parallels that of Paul in 1 Cor. 2:9, as well as in the Gospel of Thomas and other texts from the Nag Hammadi library. Marvin Meyer, Rodolphe Kasser, Marvin Meyer, and Gregor Wurst, eds., "Judas and the Gnostic Connection," in *The Gospel of Judas* (Washington, DC: National Geographic Society, 2006), 144–45.

> For gnostics, a person is not saved by having faith in Christ or doing good works. Rather, a person is saved by knowing the truth—the truth about the world we live in, about who the true God is, and especially about who we are ourselves. In other words, this is largely *self-knowledge*. [Emphasis added.]

This self-knowledge is key to the Gnostic Gospels. In the *Book of Thomas the Contender*, Jesus says to Thomas, called his twin brother: "For he who has not known himself has known nothing, but he who has known himself has at the same time already achieved knowledge about the depth of the All." In the *Gospel of Thomas*, Jesus is quoted as saying, "Rather, the Kingdom is inside of you, and it is outside of you. When you come to know yourselves, then you will be known, and you will realize that you are the sons of the living Father. But if you will not know yourselves, then you will dwell in poverty, and it is you yourself who are that poverty." The *Gospel of Thomas* also states, "If you bring forth what is in you, what you bring forth will save you. If you do not bring forth what is in you, what you do not bring forth will kill you." Silvanus tells his students, "Before everything else, . . . know yourself." And in the *Testimony of Truth*, "When man comes to know himself and God who is over the truth, he will be saved, and he will crown himself with the crown unfading."

The process of coming to "know thyself" is not, according to the *Gospel of Thomas*, an easy one. "Jesus said, 'Let one who seeks not stop seeking until one finds. When one finds, one will be disturbed. When he becomes disturbed, one will be amazed and will reign over all.'" Also in the *Gospel of Thomas*, "Blessed is one who has suffered: that one has found life." This difficult process is an alchemical one that occurs within: "When you make the two into one, when you make the inner like the outer and the outer like the inner, and the upper like the lower, when you make male and female into a single one . . . then you will enter the Kingdom."[28] According to Silvanus, one must "knock upon

---

[28] Segal notes that, "The 'secret knowledge' necessary for eternal life can be interpreted as gaining self-knowledge through unification. The emphasis on salvation by self-knowledge suggests that the terms 'male and female' are used metaphorically in the Thomas sayings to represent aspects of the

yourself as upon a door and walk upon yourself as on a straight road. For if you walk upon the road, it is impossible for you to go astray . . . Open the door for yourself that you may know what is . . . Whatever you will open for yourself, you will open."

Regarding the ancient maxim "Know thyself," Gurdjieff tells us,

> These words . . . which are generally ascribed to Socrates, actually lie at the basis of many systems and schools far more ancient than the Socratic. But although modern thought is aware of the existence of this principle it has only a very vague idea of its meaning and significance. The ordinary man of our times, even a man with philosophic or scientific interests, does not realize that the principle "know thyself" speaks of the necessity of knowing one's machine, the "human machine."[29]

Gurdjieff tells his students that to awaken, to "know thyself," requires an understanding of the human machine. "Without self-knowledge, without understanding the working and functioning of his machine, man cannot be free, he cannot govern himself and he will always remain a slave, the plaything of forces acting upon him." Ouspensky explains further, "We live and act and reason in deep sleep, not metaphorically but in absolute reality . . . at the same time, we *can remember ourselves* if we make sufficient efforts, that [is] we *can awaken*." [Emphasis added.]

---

individual personality." Segal, 475, *citing*, Wayne A. Meeks, "The Image of the Androgyne: Some Uses of a Symbol in Earliest Christianity, *History of Religion*, Vol. 13, No. 3 (1974), 165–208.

[29] Gurdjieff tells us, "Man is a machine. All his deeds, actions, words, thoughts, feelings, convictions, opinions, and habits are the results of external influences." *Search*, 21. He explains further, "Man such as we know him, the 'man-machine,' the man who cannot 'do' and with whom and through whom everything 'happens,' cannot have a permanent and single I. His I changes as quickly as his thoughts, feelings, moods, and he makes a profound mistake in considering himself always one and the same person. . . . Every thought, every mood, every sensation, says 'I.'" *Search*, 59.

Thus, the first stage of the path to immortality is to *awaken*. "To awake, to die, to be born, these are three successive stages." Gurdjieff told his students,

> There is nothing new in the idea of sleep. People have been told almost since the creation of the world that they are asleep and that they must awaken. How many times is this said in the Gospels, for instance? "Awake," "watch," "sleep not." Christ's disciples even slept when he was praying in the Garden of Gethsemane for the last time. It is all there. But do men understand it? Men take it simply as a form of speech, as an expression, as a metaphor. They completely fail to understand that it must be taken literally.

Among the themes shared by the Gnostic gospels is this need to "awaken." Various figures of speech are used to describe this state: "asleep, drunk, ignorant, in darkness." In the *Teachings of Silvanus*, Silvanus admonishes his students, "End the sleep which lays heavily upon you. Depart from the oblivion which fills you with darkness. . . . Why do you pursue the darkness, though the light is available for you?" In the *Gospel of Truth*, Jesus is described as the teacher who "enlightened those who were in darkness through forgetfulness [i.e., they did not remember themselves]. He enlightened them and showed them a way. The way, then, is the truth which he taught them." According to the *Gospel of Thomas*, Jesus stated that when He came to this world, "I found them all drunk, and I did not find any of them thirsty. My soul ached for these human children, because they are blind of heart and do not see, that they came into the world empty, and they also seek to depart from the world empty. But now they are drunk. When they become sober, then they will repent."

Another theme among the Gnostics is that there is a death—which is not a physical death—that precedes and is necessary in order to attain salvation (immortality). The *Secret Book of James* states, "Therefore, become seekers of death . . . Verily I say unto you, none of those who fear death will be saved, for the kingdom belongs to those who put themselves to death."

When asked by a student, "In what sense was it said that one who has not died cannot be born?" Gurdjieff responded,

All religions speak about death during this life on earth. Death must come before rebirth. But what must die? False confidence in one's own knowledge, self-love and egoism. Our egoism must be broken. We must realize that we are very complicated machines, and so this process of breaking is bound to be a long and difficult task. Before real growth becomes possible, our personality must die.

Thus, in order to be born—to create a soul—one must first awaken, that is, realize that he or she "is going nowhere and does not know where to go," then die to the *false* personality, that is, free oneself "from a thousand petty attachments and identifications." Only if one awakens and dies to the false personality is it possible to be born and grow a soul.

As noted in chapter one, in this process of awakening, dying and giving birth to a soul, a person develops higher spiritual bodies. Gurdjieff explains,

> According to an ancient teaching, traces of which may be found in many systems, old and new, a man who has attained the full development possible for man, a man in the full sense of the word, *consists of four bodies.* These four bodies are composed of substances which gradually become finer and finer, mutually interpenetrate one another, and form four independent organisms, standing in a definite relationship to one another but capable of independent action. [Emphasis in original.]

These four bodies are defined in different teachings in various ways, which Gurdjieff captured in a diagram for his students, reproduced below.

1st body	2nd body	3rd body	4th body
Carnal body	Natural body	Spiritual body	Divine body
"Carriage" (body)	"Horse" (feelings, desires)	"Driver" (mind)	"Master" (I, consciousness, will)
Physical body	Astral body	Mental body	Causal body

Gurdjieff explains that the first is the physical body, in Christian terminology the "carnal" body; the second, in Christian terminology, is the natural body; the third is the "spiritual" body; and the fourth, in the terminology of *esoteric Christianity*, is the "divine" body." In certain Eastern religions, the first body is the carriage (body), the second is the horse (feelings, desires), the third the driver (mind), and the fourth the master (I, consciousness, will). In theosophical terminology, the first is the "physical" body, the second is the "astral," the third is the "mental," and the fourth the "causal." Gurdjieff tells us that parallels may be found in most systems and teachings that recognize something more in man than the physical body. Certain esoteric teachings compare this development of the spiritual potential in human beings to a house with four rooms:

> Man lives in one room, the smallest and poorest of all, and until he is told of it, he does not suspect the existence of the other rooms which are full of treasures. When he does learn of this he begins to seek the keys of these rooms and especially of the fourth, the most important, room. And when a man has found his way into this room, he really has become the master of his house, for only then does the house belong to him wholly and forever.

Whatever the nomenclature, Gurdjieff stressed that "almost all these teachings, while repeating in a more or less familiar form the definitions and divisions of the ancient teaching, have forgotten or omitted its most important feature, which is: *that man is not born with the finer bodies*, and that they can only be artificially cultivated in him provided favorable conditions both internal and external are present." [Emphasis added.] And all esoteric religious teachings make clear that the development of the finer higher bodies can only be acquired after great effort and great labor. Gurdjieff went on to say,

> Only the man who possesses four fully developed bodies can be called a "man" in the full sense of the word. This man possesses many properties which ordinary man does not possess. *One of these properties is immortality.* All religions and all ancient teachings contain the idea that, by acquiring

the fourth body, man acquires immortality; and they all contain indications of the ways to acquire the fourth body, that is, immortality. [Emphasis in original.]

Remarkably, this teaching of the development of the higher bodies can be found in the *esoteric* teachings of Paul. Understood through Alan Segal's meticulous translation of Paul's carefully constructed words, *soma psychikon* and *soma pneumatikon*, the letters of Paul reveal numerous references to the development of higher bodies. As we will see, since the discovery of the Nag Hammadi library, it has also become clear that several Gnostic sects, the Valentinians and Naassenes in particular, revered Paul and claimed that their secret tradition offered "direct access to Paul's *own* teaching of wisdom and gnosis." [Emphasis in original.] That is, Paul taught his disciples the teachings of *esoteric* Christianity.[30]

The Esoteric Teachings of Paul & The Fourth Way

While orthodox Christian theologians, both ancient and modern, laud Paul as an anti-gnostic, an opponent of the "gnostic heresy," and dismiss the secret nature of Paul's teachings, the Gnostic poet Valentinus claimed that he himself learned Paul's secret teaching from Theudas, one of Paul's disciples. Valentinus, whose enemies spoke of him as a brilliant and eloquent man, is believed to have authored *The Gospel of Truth*, as well as the *Tripartite Tractate* and *Interpretation of the Gnosis*. "According to Valentinus, there are esoteric teachings which originate from Jesus that were passed on in secret. When Jesus spoke in public, He used metaphors that did not disclose His complete teachings. He only

---

[30] Eastern Orthodox theology teaches that the body and soul are a single whole, as opposed to the soul being separate from and "imprisoned in" the body, and that the body as well as the soul must be transfigured or "deified." In the mystical, ascetic tradition of Eastern Orthodoxy, the goal is to "become god, to attain *theosis*, 'deification' or 'divination,'" which can be achieved through the "prayer of silence" or "inner stillness." Ware, 64. "The human person, when deified, remains distinct (though not separate) from God.... [and] the body will share with the soul in unspeakable blessings." *See* Ware, 231–33.

passed them on to his disciples in private. He referred to this when He said: 'The knowledge about the secrets of the kingdom of heaven has been given to you, but to the rest it comes by means of parables so that they may look but not see and listen but not understand.'"

In her book *The Gnostic Paul*, Elaine Pagels points out that it was among the Valentinians that "Paul's 'mysticism' has been received with the greatest favor and used in a more or less systematic fashion . . . the work [*The Gospel of Truth*, attributed to Valentinus] is permeated from beginning to end with allusions to the Pauline corpus." The Valentinians claimed Paul's letters as the source of "their anthropology, their Christology, and their sacramental theology." They also claimed that Paul taught "in two ways at once," and that

> only those who have received initiation into [their] secret, oral tradition are capable of understanding the true meaning of the scriptures—which include Paul's letters . . . The Valentinians claim that most Christians make the mistake of reading the scriptures only literally. They themselves, through their initiation into gnosis, learn to read his letters (as they read all scripture) on the symbolic level, as they say Paul intended.

Thus, the Valentinians insisted, it is only through "living speech," not written documents, that truth can be transmitted.

The followers of Valentinus called themselves *pneumatics*. They distinguished between *pneumatic* Christians initiated into the secret oral tradition, i.e., the "elect," and *psychic* orthodox Christians with "simple-minded faith" who read the scriptures literally, i.e., the "called." As Pagels explains, the Valentinians understood Paul's discussion of Jews and Gentiles in Romans 2 allegorically, as referring to the two different groups of Christians—the Jews were the *psychics*, the Gentiles the *pneumatics*. This completely changes what is normally understood to be the meaning of Paul's statement that he is the "Apostle to the Gentiles." Likewise, Paul's oft-quoted (and widely reviled) passage from Ephesians, "The women are subject to their own men as to the Lord; for the man is the head of the woman, as also Christ is the head of the Church," is understood by the Valentinians as referring metaphorically to the *psychics* as "women" and the *pneumatics* as "men." Thus, when

Paul refers to "the female becoming male," he is speaking of the *psychics* becoming *pneumatic*—that is, coming to possess the fourth body of which Gurdjieff speaks, a pneumatic and immortal body like that of Christ.

Using Alan Segal's translations, it is possible to trace the *esoteric* meaning of the language of Paul regarding the *development* of the higher spiritual body. As noted in chapter three, Paul uses the term *soma psychikon*, the combined body and soul of the Greeks, to describe the ordinary body, the body of the *psychics*, according to the Valentinians. In contrast, Paul uses the term *soma pneumatikon* to describe the higher body, the body sought by the *pneumatics*, that is, "the ordinary body subsumed and transformed by the spirit. This new, spiritual, glorious body which . . . is equivalent to Christ's body."

Critical to understanding that the fourth body, i.e., the immortal soul, must be developed is Segal's analysis of Paul's language regarding *transformation*. In Philippians, Paul speaks of "becoming like him [Jesus] in his death (*symmorphizomeno toi thantoi autou*)." Later, he says, "But our commonwealth is in heaven, and from it we await a Savior, the Lord Jesus Christ, who will change (*metaschematisei*) our lowly body to be conformed in shape (*symmorphon*) to his glorious body (*toi somati tes doxes autou*) by the power that enables him even to subject all things to himself."

Segal tells us that we do not have a word in English to capture the meaning of the Greek *symmorphizomeno:*

> If we had an English word for it, it would be *symmorphosis,* like "metamorphosis" but with a more intimate and transformative meaning. The Greek word means literally "to be morphed together with," what our word "metamorphosize" suggests, except that it states that the reformation will explicitly take place "together with" (*sym-*) his glorious body, suggesting the outcome is a new compound of both. The body of the believer eventually is to be transformed together with and combined into the body of Christ. The believer's body is to be changed into the same spiritual body of glory as that of the savior.

And, Segal states, we would need to coin another new word to understand the meaning of the Greek *metaschematisei*, which means "to change the structure of," because the English translation does not capture the full meaning in the Greek. By using this word, Paul was suggesting that this transformation from "lowly body to His glorious body 'metaschematizes,' creates a 'metascheme.'" The new structure refers to the higher bodies that must be developed to create a soul, bodies composed of finer and finer substances, mutually interpenetrating yet independent. The fourth body, the divine or spiritual body, is that which has metaschematized (*metaschematisei*), that is, changed its structure, to be conformed in shape (*symmorphon*) with that of Christ's divine body. Segal explains that the word *symmorphon* suggests a "spiritual reformation of the believer's body into the form of the divine image." As Segal says, "it all depends on a notion of body that is a *new spiritualized substance*, a new body which is not flesh and blood." [Emphasis added.]

Segal tells us,

> This new, spiritual, glorious body, which is the redeemed, resurrected body, is equivalent to Christ's body.
>
> . . . They [the *pneumatics*] warrant immortality because they have been transformed by becoming formed like (*symmorphous*) the savior.

Thus, Paul's statement, "It is sown a physical body [*soma psychikon*], it is raised a spiritual body [*soma pneumatikon*]," takes on new meaning. Paul teaches that instead of the separation of the immortal soul from the physical body, i.e., death of the *soma psychikon* as the Greeks understood it, immortality would be achieved by transforming the physical body into the *soma pneumatikon*, the *pneumatic* or spiritual body, which is "the natural body augmented and divine, a new spiritualized substance." Paul tells his followers that the physical body will put on immortality as a garment and be transformed by it. As Segal notes, Paul

> developed a notion of a self in transformation which attained transcendent status at the end of time but was continuously realizing it in the present. So while it was the body that is resurrected it was not merely the body; it was the body

which included a divine consciousness, the Spirit which was redeeming the world. It was a picture of the self that said one could remake the world from what it is into what it should be, *all by perfecting the self.* [Emphasis added.]

Needless to say, this is a completely different view of the resurrection than that of the church fathers.

Segal notes with surprise that according to Paul, this transformation was to be effected by being transformed in Christ *in his death* (*symmorphizomenos toi thanatou autou*, Phil. 3:10) and that the identification with the death of Christ is a crucial issue for understanding Paul's experience. But as Pagels points out, a key theme in Paul, as well as for the Valentinians, was defining "baptism 'as dying with Christ.'" Segal does not draw the connection between Paul's statement and the esoteric death of which Paul speaks. But as Gurdjieff says,

> It is just this death that is spoken of in all religions. It is defined in the saying that has reached us from remote antiquity, "Without death no resurrection," that is to say, "If you do not die, you will not be resurrected." The death referred to is not the death of the body, since for such death there is no need for resurrection. For if there is a soul, and moreover, an immortal soul, it can dispense with a resurrection of the body. Nor is the necessity of resurrection our appearance before the awful Judgment of the Lord God, as we have been taught by the Fathers of the Church. No! Even Jesus Christ and all the other prophets sent from Above spoke of the death which might occur even during life, that is to say, of the death of the "Tyrant" from whom proceeds our slavery in this life and solely from the liberation from which depends the first chief liberation of man.

This "tyrant" is the sleep of egoism, the ignorance that enslaves human beings. For as Pagels explains, to the Gnostics, sleep is "the oblivion of the soul," and when the "savior comes he shines as light *to awaken the soul and resurrect the dead.*" [Emphasis added.]

It was not only the Valentinians among the Gnostics who recognized the significance of the body. In the *Gospel of Thomas*, Jesus is quoted as saying, "Whoever has come to know the world has discovered the body, and whoever has discovered the body is worth more than the world." The *Dialogue of the Savior* states, "If one does not understand how the body that he wears came to be, he will perish with it . . . Whoever does not understand how he came will not understand how he will go." Other Gnostic texts also provide descriptions of the soul quite different from the orthodox Christian understanding. For example, in the *Secret Book of John*, Jesus is quoted as saying that those who are interested exclusively in the imperishable will have their souls empowered by the Spirit of Life and live eternally. Yet those in whom the contemptible spirit lives will have their souls chained until they emerge from forgetfulness and acquire knowledge allowing them to achieve perfection and be saved. The way of redemption is described: "The soul needs to follow another soul in whom the Spirit of Life dwells, because she is saved through the Spirit. Then she will never be thrust into flesh again."

The Gospel of Judas

There is another Gnostic Gospel that has striking parallels to the teachings of Gurdjieff. As noted above, in 2001 the *Gospel of Judas* was rediscovered after having first been found in the 1970s then pirated by antiquities brokers for three decades. The *Gospel of Judas* provides an account of Judas's role that radically alters the historical view of Judas as the great betrayer of Jesus. As Pagels describes, "The *Gospel of Judas* shows Judas instead as Jesus's closest and most trusted confidant—the one to whom Jesus reveals his deepest mysteries and whom he trusts to initiate the passion." Meyers tells us that Judas "betrays Jesus in the *Gospel of Judas*, but he does so knowingly, at the sincere request of Jesus." Remarkably, Gurdjieff told the same story of Judas Iscariot in *All and Everything*, which he began writing in the mid-1920s and worked on for the next two decades. It was published in 1950, not long after Gurdjieff died in October of 1949, approximately twenty years before the *Gospel of Judas* was found by peasants near Al Minya in Middle Egypt.

In *All and Everything*, Gurdjieff describes Judas as "this devoted and favorite Apostle initiated by Jesus Christ Himself." Judas was "not only the most faithful and devoted of all the near followers of Jesus Christ, but also, only thanks to his Reason and presence of mind all the acts of the Sacred

Individual [Jesus] . . ." were completed, allowing Jesus to fulfill His sacred mission. Because Jesus did not have the necessary time before He was crucified to instruct His apostles in certain cosmic truths, Gurdjieff tells us He had to resort to a sacred ceremony so that He might complete His mission while still in a cosmic individual state. It was just here that Judas put forward an ingenious plan—the conscious betrayal of Christ—that would gain them the necessary time. Gurdjieff refers to Judas as a saint, the most devoted of all His disciples, who had the highest degree of reason.

In the *Gospel of Judas*, Judas sees Jesus more clearly than the other disciples, recognizing His divine origin; Jesus then takes Judas aside to reveal the secret teaching. Jesus says, "I shall tell you the mysteries of the kingdom. It is possible for you to reach it, but you will grieve a great deal. For someone else will replace you, in order that the twelve [disciples] may again come to completion with their god."

As interpreted by Bart Ehrman, in the *Gospel of Judas*, when Judas handed Jesus over to the authorities, he "performed the greatest service imaginable" by enabling Jesus "to escape his own mortal flesh and return to his eternal home." Ehrman notes that Jesus tells Judas, "You will exceed all of them. For you will sacrifice the man that clothes me." Even greater than assisting Jesus with His physical death, however, Gurdjieff explains that Judas made possible the esoteric ceremony that took place during the Last Supper, allowing Jesus to communicate with His disciples after His crucifixion. Gurdjieff says it was "this Judas, now a Saint and formerly the inseparable and devoted helper of Jesus Christ and who is 'hated' and 'cursed' owning to the naïve unreasonableness [of human begins] . . . who rendered his great objective service . . . [for which] all subsequent generations should be grateful." [31]

---

[31] Of interest to students of The Fourth Way, Segal draws connections to *self-remembering* by noting that, regarding the Last Supper, Paul told his disciples, "the ritual is to be enacted 'in remembrance of me.'" Segal went on to state, "Paul found remembrance (*anamnesis*) to be the basis of his spiritual life in Christ. But remembrance is something that takes place in the mind as part of a liturgical event. It is not the event alone which makes the ritual effective, because Paul described ways in which the liturgical moment could be violated by improper behavior. He said one must 'examine oneself' and 'discern the body' in the ritual, meaning the perception of the reality of the body of Christ is partly the responsibility of the participant." Segal, 443.

Kiss of Judas (Giotti)

The *Gospel of Judas* also contains a surprising reference to two types of souls. One is "a gift," an immortal soul, the other "on loan." The soul on loan is not immortal but is merely the "breath of life." Jesus tells Judas, "The souls of every human generation will die. When these people [those with the gift], however, have completed their time of the kingdom and the spirit [breath of life] leaves them, their bodies will die but their souls will be alive, and they will be taken up." Similarly, Gurdjieff references this "soul on loan," distinguishing it from the immortal soul. In his writings, he refers to the soul on loan as "soul," contrasting it to the immortal soul, which is referred to without the use of quotation marks. He explains the role of the "soul" on loan in the Megalocosmos:

> Everything living sets free at its death a certain amount of the energy that has "animated" it; this energy, or the "souls" of everything living—plants, animals, people—is attracted to the moon as though by a huge electromagnet, and brings to it the warmth and the life upon which its growth depends,

that is, the growth of the ray of creation. In the economy of the universe nothing is lost, and a certain energy having finished its work on one plane goes to another.

Thus, in the *Gospel of Judas*, as well as in a number of other Gnostic Gospels, what at first appears to contradict Gurdjieff's teaching that we do not have an immortal soul is, in fact, consistent with his explanation of what happens at death. That is, the animating energy of human beings who do not crystallize the substances necessary to form a soul are released for use in the Megaloscosmos: "If a man has begun to accumulate these substances, but dies before they have crystallized, then simultaneously with the death of the physical body, these substances also disintegrate and become dispersed." Therefore, those who have not crystallized a soul have no self-consciousness inherent in those animating substances—that is, they are mortal.

As we have seen, a number of the Gnostic Gospels ground their teachings on the soul in the *esoteric* teaching of Paul. As such, they reveal Paul's secret teaching of the necessity to transform the ordinary physical body (*soma psychikon*) into the pneumatic, divine body (*soma pneumatikon*), the fourth body of esoteric Christianity of which Gurdjieff speaks. Pagels notes that like Paul, the *Gospel of Judas* rejects the resurrection of the physical body, focusing instead on the spiritual, immortal body that can be developed "even as they live in this world." In like manner, Segal points out that the *Gospel of Thomas* "parallels Paul in taking the spiritual nature of the resurrection body (*soma pneumatikon*) very seriously indeed." While we must piece together the fragments of esoteric Christianity now available in the Gnostic Gospels, as well as in the letters of Paul, The Fourth Way provides the complete teaching of esoteric Christianity. As Patterson notes, "The Fourth Way, for Gurdjieff, is *esoteric Christianity* in its highest form."

Conclusion

From its very beginnings, the religion that became known as Christianity was grounded in an ancient teaching that preceded even the philosophers of antiquity. That Augustine himself acknowledged this at the end of his life, noting that "what is now called the Christian religion existed of old and was never absent from the beginning of the human race until Christ came in the flesh," is remarkable. Yet this ancient teaching is not visible in the Christianity we know today, exoteric Christianity. Rather, it is the hidden, esoteric Christianity taught by Jesus, which is preserved in the works of the esoteric Paul and the Gnostics and which dates back, as we've seen, to pre-sand Egypt.

Unlike exoteric Christianity, which holds that we are each born with an immortal soul, esoteric Christianity, kept deliberately hidden from the uninitiated, teaches that we do not have a soul but may develop one. This can be found through a careful translation of Paul's language, which allows us to grasp the precise meaning of the terms he coined to describe the creation of a higher divine body composed of a "new spiritualized substance." The creation of this body is done through a process Segal translates from Paul as "self-perfecting."

As we also have seen, Paul's teaching and that of several schools of Gnosticism parallel The Fourth Way teaching that to develop an immortal soul, we must create higher bodies made of finer and finer substances. The Fourth Way teaches us *how* to do this—through the processes of *self-sensing, self-remembering,* and *self-observation.* That is, through what Paul calls "self-perfecting," a term Gurdjieff also uses, clarifying that it is self-perfecting in the sense of imperishable Being. Key to this process is the development of "self-knowledge," an understanding of what Gurdjieff calls the human machine. This is the self-knowledge at the heart of the ancient saying, "Know thyself." In order to attain self-knowledge, we must first awaken to the fact we are asleep, then die to what is false within us. Through this process of self-perfecting, we create the finer substances within the physical body necessary to create the higher-being bodies and so grow an immortal soul.

AFTERWORD

AFTER YOU DIE—*WHAT?*

For most people, unfortunately, the answer is . . . *nothing*. This answer we immediately reject. It seems so unfair. But ask: from what is this judgment's origin? Isn't it from our level, the level of the human being? But what about nature? From nature's point of view, we are simply part of organic life on the earth. We've been given birth simply to receive, process and transmit energies, and to procreate. All this happens mechanically. So the answer, though harsh and impersonal from our perspective, is lawful.

The writer Aldous Huxley, author of *Brave New World*, understood this reality. Writing in the mid-twentieth century, he said,

> Madness consists, for example, of thinking of oneself as a soul, a coherent and enduring human entity. But, between the animal below and the spirit above, there is nothing on the human level except a swarm of constellated impulses and sentiments and notions; a swarm brought together by the accidents of heredity and language; a swarm of incongruous and often contradictory thoughts and desires. Memory and the slowly changing body constitute a kind of spatiotemporal cage, within which the swarm is enclosed. To talk of it as if it were a coherent and enduring "soul" is madness. On the human level there is no such thing as a soul.

But we don't have to die without a soul. Fortunately, unlike one- and two-centered beings, as three-centered beings we are "the image of

God," as Mr. Gurdjieff says; and so we have the possibility to create a soul from "a cloud of fine matters or energies connected together and bound to the physical body." It is the repeated fusion of these over time that crystallizes that which can survive bodily death—a soul.

How to Create a Soul

How do we create a soul? For that, it is necessary to be present, to integrate body-sense-mind. As we live in change, is there anything in us that can withstand external and internal influences? If not, there is nothing in us that can survive bodily death. But if we become independent of external and internal influences, there appears in us something that can live by itself; this something may not die. In ordinary circumstances, we die every moment. Circumstances change, and the "I-of-the-moment" changes with them. If we develop in ourselves a permanent I, independent of circumstances, it can survive the death of the physical body. "The whole secret is that one cannot work for a future life without working for this one." As Gurdjieff says, if a man "becomes master of his life, he may become master of his death."

No one will dispute that the story of our life ends in death. While we have no choice but to accept this fact on an intellectual level, we reject it on an emotional one. The question of the soul and the purpose of life we can ignore until our final breath. Or we can grow a soul.

Gurdjieff distinguishes the fate of a person who develops a permanent I and becomes master of his life from one who does not develop his own I. To understand this distinction more fully, Gurdjieff gave a lecture in which he employed the metaphor of life as a river in which each of us lives as a single drop of water.

Involution or Conscious Evolution?

Initially, from its source, the river flows along a level valley, but due to a cataclysm, the river divides into two separate streams. One stream flows into the vast ocean, where it participates in evolutionary processes; the other ultimately seeps into the very depths of the earth, where the drops of water are transformed into steam and "distributed into corresponding spheres of new arising."

Thus, the dividing of the river leads to two possibilities: A drop of water (i.e., a person) that engages in inner subjective "struggles of one's own self-denial" might develop an "I" enabling it to flow, at the point the river divides, into the evolutionary stream. This evolutionary stream empties into the vast ocean, where there is a "reciprocal exchange of substances between various great cosmic concentrations," giving the drop of water the possibility to evolve to the "next higher concentration." Those that fail to engage in any inner struggle enter the involutionary flow of the river. In that stream, life has a totally accidental character: the direction, movement, and states of the drop of water are caused by its different positions within the river, which are in turn caused by various accidental surrounding conditions and the tempo of the river's current.

Our difficulty is that, as adults, we are now past the point where the river branches, and we remain unaware of our situation as we passively flow in the involutionary stream, along with nearly everyone else. Because we are in the involutionary stream, we do not have an individual fate: "For the drops there is not a separate predetermination of their personal fate—a predetermined fate is for the whole river only."

But Gurdjieff's metaphor does not stop there. The two streams do not remain mutually independent. Even after the initial branching, the streams frequently approach so near to each other that at certain times events (winds, storms) make it possible for separate drops to pass from one river to the other. Thus, even for those drops in the involutionary stream—that is, even for us—it is possible to pass into the evolutionary stream.

The expression from ancient times, "'the first liberation of man' refers to just this possibility." However, it is not easy to make this crossing. [32] One must consciously develop a "constant unquenchable impulse of desire for such a crossing" followed by "a long corresponding preparation." To cross over, one must renounce all of what seem to be

---

[32] The difficulties are recognized in all genuine teachings. The title of Somerset Maugham's book *The Razor's Edge* is taken from a passage in the *Katha Upanishad*, a sacred Hindu text: "The sharp edge of a razor is difficult to pass over, thus the wise say the path to Salvation is hard."

our "blessings" but which are in reality our "automatically and slavishly acquired habits" present in this stream of life. This is the death that is referred to in all religions—we must die to what has become our ordinary, habitual life. The saying from ancient times is "Without death, no resurrection." But the resurrection referred to here is not the resurrection of the body, for as Gurdjieff says, "If there is a soul, and moreover an immortal soul, it can dispense with the resurrection of the body." Gurdjieff states, "Even Jesus Christ himself and all the other prophets sent from Above spoke of the death which might occur even during life, that is to say, of the death of that 'Tyrant' from whom proceeds our slavery in this life, and solely from the liberation from which depends the first chief liberation of man." This liberation is recognized in all genuine teachings, including The Fourth Way, the sacred science of ancient Egypt and esoteric Christianity. These teachings give us the possibility of crossing over into the evolutionary stream, enabling us to grow a soul, perhaps even an immortal soul.

As we've seen, this knowledge regarding the soul and the sacred science of being has existed since prehistoric Egypt. Yet today we live in a culture and era that is unconcerned with the sacred science of being. Instead, most of us assume that we have a soul, and if we are "good," we will reap our heavenly reward. Others believe they have no soul, and there is no purpose in life beyond achieving pleasure. Regardless, don't we all cling to the notion that Maugham portrayed through Isabel, Larry's one-time fiancée, that it is either awkward or pointless to talk about these things? How many people have you met who are actively engaged in pursuing these questions? We would rather view the world personally and believe that it will all turn out well in the end for us. Or we simply write off the possibility of knowing what happens to us at death.

And so we end where we began. Somerset Maugham introduced *The Razor's Edge* with a kind of apology because the book does not have a definitive ending. Maugham does not know what happened to Larry after their last conversation. As Maugham says, "I leave my readers in the air." And at the end of this book, we leave you, dear reader, in the air—for it is up to you to decide what happens. *Now* . . .

APPENDIX

ZOROASTRIANISM

All those who will give hearing for Me unto this one (the Prophet Zarathustra) will come unto Salvation and Immortality through the works of the Good Spirit.

THIS WAS THE PROMISE GIVEN BY THE GOD AHURA MAZDA, lord of life and wisdom, to those who accepted the guidance of his prophet Zarathustra, who lived in ancient Persia. The little-known religion espoused by this prophet is known today by the name Zoroastrianism (from Zoroaster, the prophet's Greek name). Though not widely known or practiced, its tenets influenced Christianity, Islam and Judaism as we know them today. [33]

---

[33] Jews were under Persian rule from 536 to 333 BCE "and their religion was subjected to the influence of Persian thought. The doctrine of the Satan... first appears in the post-exilic Books of Zechariah, Job, and Chronicles 1 and is almost certainly a reflex of the Persian Zoroastrian doctrine of Angromainyu, or Ahriman, the Evil One, the antithesis of Ahura-mazda, or Ormazd, the Good God." Lewis Bayles Paton, *Spiritism and the Cult of the Dead in Antiquity* (New York: Macmillan, 1921), 280. And as mentioned in chapter five, some believe that Zoroastrianism is at the root of some schools of Gnosticism. Elaine Pagels, *The Gnostic Gospels* (New York: Vintage Books, 1979), xxx–xxxiii. Zoroastrianism has been an inspiration to writers and

Zoroastrianism was established in what is now Iran and became the dominant religion within the Persian Empire beginning in the sixth century BCE. Although Zarathustra was said to have composed a vast literature, only a small portion remains—the *Gathas*, seventeen inspired devotional hymns, many addressed directly to God. Zarathustra's oral teachings were handed down from generation to generation and became widespread during and following his lifetime. The religion maintained a strong presence through the seventh century CE. Gradually, however, it was crushed by invasions, beginning in 330 BCE with the invasion of Alexander the Great, who ordered his army to deliberately kill Zoroastrian priests and destroy religious texts.[34] An Arabian invasion in 641 CE further decimated the religion as its adherents scattered and hid. Eventually some migrated to India, forming the Parsee community. Today followers of Zoroastrianism are few, numbering perhaps two hundred thousand worldwide.

Zarathustra's Life

Any recounting of Zarathustra's life involves a great deal of speculation. It is not known when he lived or precisely where he was born. The range of possible dates for his life is quite wide; respected scholars have found evidence that he was born as early as 1700 BCE or as late as about 500 BCE. But it does appear that the world he was living in was undergoing change, moving from the Stone Age to the Bronze Age.

---

artists—seeping into popular culture as well. *This Obscure Religion Shaped the West*, British Broadcasting Company, April 6, 2017, http://www.bbc.com/culture/story/20170406-this-obscure-religion-shaped-the-west.

[34] J. G. Bennett, in *Making a New World*, suggests that Zarathustra may be Ashiata Shiemash, whom Gurdjieff describes as one of the Messengers from Above. J. G. Bennett, *Making a New World* (Santa Fe, NM: Bennett Books, 1992), 46. Gurdjieff writes that Alexander deliberately destroyed evidence of the teachings of Ashiata Shiemash, who was the only Messenger who succeeded in creating on earth, "conditions in which the existence of its unfortunate beings somewhat resembled for a certain time the existence of the three-brained beings of the other planets of our great Universe." *All and Everything*, 348, 404, 423.

Before the advent of the Bronze Age, the Indo-Iranians lived in a static society of nomadic and semi-nomadic herders and hunters. They had not yet domesticated horses, so travel was limited and groups of people lived in relative isolation. The focus of their pre-Zoroastrian religious practices was the maintenance of cosmic order with rituals, sacrifices and adherence to a moral code to ensure that new life replaced the old. The principle of *Asha*, the natural law that maintained order and the continuity of existence, also provided guidance for human behavior through its moral values of truth and righteousness. Following death, the spirit of the deceased was believed to live in a subterranean kingdom, and certain rituals carried out by the living relatives were thought to help the spirit avoid evil powers and reach the dwelling place of the great company of the dead. The way one lived one's life, however, did not seem to impact whether the spirit reached the sought-after destination.

Values shifted under the influence of new technologies and methods of transportation. As the Indo-Iranians moved south and came into contact with Mesopotamians, they learned to domesticate horses and employ bronze to make weapons and build chariots. That change in technology brought its own degenerating influences. The stability of life based on herding and its focus on cosmic maintenance gave way to raiding and pillaging, as respect for the rule of law gave way to warriors' desires for riches and glory. Society divided into those who sought to follow *Asha* and adherents of *drujvants*, the wicked ones, creating disorder. To support the warring behavior, new gods with new values were created; chief among them was *Indra*, amoral but loyal and generous to those who revered him.

As a young priest, Zarathustra was apparently troubled by the lawlessness and violence. At the age of thirty, he had a visionary experience in which he was led into the presence of Ahura Mazda and six other radiant beings, collectively called the *heptad*. From this experience, his purpose in life was ordained: to teach others to seek *Asha*. "As long as I have the will and the strength, so long will I preach the search for Truth."

Zoroastrianism & the Soul

A fundamental tenet of Zoroastrianism is that every person has a soul, the fate of which depends on the choices made during one's lifetime. In the *Avesta*, the holy scripture of Zoroastrianism, human beings are seen as being both part of and distinct from nature. The part of us that is of nature dies, inevitably submitting to the laws of nature. The part that is immaterial is not subject to the laws of nature and can achieve immortality. But for this to happen, for us to achieve self-perfection during our lifetime, we must make right efforts, carrying out daily and annual rituals with right intention and truly spoken words. In so doing, the person continues God's work of creation. This way to immortality is expressed in the precept "good thoughts, good words, good deeds." Through adherence to this moral code, and through both utilization of and submission to the laws of nature, human beings can overcome gravitation, the reign of death, which leads to the breakup of the organism into its inorganic components. If a person develops higher vibrations within and concomitantly higher mental currents, he or she will acquire greater understanding of, and union with, the eternal forces. As stated in a *Gatha*,

> I declare to you what the Most Benevolent One said to me: "My word is the best for mortals to hear. They who will offer willing obedience to My Word will advance towards Perfection and Immortality. Mazda is the Lord of actions inspired by the Good Mind."

Choice is an important component of Zoroastrianism. A person hears the prophet's word and makes choices through the use of the various inner faculties given for this purpose, either utilizing them or allowing them to remain dormant. These faculties include our physical bodies, conscience, intelligence, and two types of what may be called mental energy: *Khratu*, allowing directive intelligence, and *Chisti*, the feminine counterpart, which enables one to penetrate deeply, permitting insight leading to enlightenment. The final and important capacity we are given is *Sraosha*, the inner capacity to be still and listen to the voice of Ahura Mazda within us. *Sraosha*, which is also a form of discipline, is always accompanied by *Ashi Vanghui*, the material and spiritual wealth that comes to one who dedicates oneself to Ahura Mazda.

Zarathustra's One God

Central to the teaching he brought was the story of cosmic creation and purpose. In a departure from past beliefs about the gods, Zarathustra proclaimed that Ahura Mazda was the one uncreated creator. The precise relationship between Ahura Mazda and the other members of the heptad is not clear, but it appears that Zarathustra came to see the six as hypostatizing attributes of the one god. Of the six Holy Immortals, the one who leads the way is Vohu Manah, "Good Purpose," and his closest ally, Asha Vahista, "Best Righteousness," personifying the principle of Asha. Zarathustra refers in the *Gathas*, his holy hymns, to Asha Vahista more than any other. These two, with the other four—Holy Devotion, Desirable Dominion, Health and Long Life—represent characteristics that can be bestowed on those who rightly venerate these qualities. What Zarathustra brought as a teaching and a set of beliefs may seem somewhat familiar to today's readers, but to those living in his time, the ideas were new and addressed the depravity of that era.

Zarathustra does not answer the question that naturally arises: How did evil enter if the benevolent Ahura Mazda is the only uncreated creator? He simply posited the existence of Ahura Mazda's twin, Angra Mainyu, also uncreated. The existence of an evil god provided some reasoned explanation for humanity's suffering. In addition, the existence of the two gods and the contrasting choices they make parallel what each of us must contend with: choices leading either to life or "not-life."

One partial explanation for the existence of evil is that when Ahura Mazda created light, he also cast his shadow and created Angra Mainyu, Death. And as Ahura Mazda created each virtue—preservation, eternal life, wisdom, work, love, peace, power, food, health, man, joy, sun, water, air, earth—the evil one created its opposite or inferior version.

Creation through Opposition

Zoroastrianism's creation story is that Ahura Mazda first created the disembodied spirit world, called *menog*. Then he gave it material existence, *getig*. The blending of the two is the act of creation that bestows the spiritual with a sentient form. Put another way, the creation of good cannot be achieved without the creation of evil. It has been said that the spirit of Good and the spirit of Evil are the twin sons of the fundamental principal of Zarvana Arakana or Limitless Time, conflict being necessary for creation and evolution. The eternal conflict of these two spirits in the universe and in the soul of humanity creates life, and so both are equally important. The existence of both allows for the recognition of each. "Without Good how can evil be recognized? Without Evil how can we know what is Good? The Zoroastrian belief is that by learning to recognize, understand and appease evil, "we can better deal with its influence both within ourselves and in others." The consequences for humanity are apparent: It has a role in exercising choice that will determine if good or evil ultimately prevails. Zarathustra's teaching inverted the worldview of his time. Instead of being pawns of the gods, who required propitiation to maintain order, mankind was working in tandem with one of the two influences affecting the outcome of this battle between the gods of good and evil.

Not only do a person's choices influence this battle, they also determine the person's ultimate fate. Zarathustra taught that upon death, the soul of the just person sits at the corpse's head for three days, chanting certain *Gathas*, invoking for itself the wished-for things. On the first night, anticipating what is to come, "the soul feels as much joy as all that it had felt in life." By contrast, the soul of the wicked person scuttles about the body of the corpse for three days, chanting "To what land to flee. Whither shall I go to flee?" and feeling as much distress as all that it had felt in life. On the fourth day, each soul meets its fate. The soul crosses the Chinvat Bridge, the Bridge of Judgment. The evil ones are separated from the good—for them the bridge is only the width of a razor, and they fall into the abyss of hell: "The conscience of the wicked man destroys for himself the reality of Truth. His soul shall torment him with retributive vengeance at the Bridge of the Separator, the Bridge of Judgment, for his own deeds and his tongue strayed from the path of truth." The wicked man steps into endless darkness, where another man questions him, but Angra Mainyu intervenes, snarling, "You shall not question him." He is given poisonous food and poisonous-smelling things, the food for a man of bad thought, bad word, bad act, bad inner self—that is, for "one not ruled by a master."

For the righteous man, the bridge is nine spear lengths wide, and a beautiful maiden, his own *Daena*, inner self/conscience, leads him across. As the soul proceeds across the bridge, he is questioned by another just man who had died before him, but Ahura Mazda intervenes, saying, "You shall not question him. He whom you question has come hither on a grim, fearful, calamitous road, that is, the separation of body and consciousness." He is brought the food for a man of good thought, good word, good act, and good inner self—for "one ruled by a master." Both the good and the evil live out this existence until the Final Judgment.

That time was moving toward a final judgment represented another radical break with the then-prevailing view—that time is circular. Zarathustra saw time moving in a linear fashion through three stages: creation, mixture and separation. The specific ending he envisioned had to do with the outcome of the struggle between good and evil. Good triumphs in the battle called *Frashokereti*, "making glorious." When good prevails, a final judgment is rendered over the earth. Fire will melt all the metals in the mountains, and the molten river will flow over the earth. All humankind will pass through this river. For the righteous, the river will be as warm milk. For the wicked, it will feel as if he is walking in the flesh through molten metal, and he will be destroyed forever. The river will flow down into hell, destroying Angra Mainyu, burning up evil in its entirety. Thus, although unable to explain the origins of evil, Zoroastrianism sees its eradication as inevitable resulting in a physical life on earth where immortality will be conferred on the resurrected bodies of the good who will be one in thought, word and deed— restored to their original perfection.

> So understand, O mortal men, the Decrees which Mazda has established regarding happiness and misery, there will be a long period of suffering for the wicked, and salvation for the just, but thereafter eternal bliss shall prevail everywhere.

JOHN MILTON, THE MORTALISTS & THE SOUL

IN HIS BOOK *JOURNEY THROUGH THIS WORLD*, C. S. Nott describes a conversation with Denis Saurat, a scholar of the poet Milton, not long after the untimely death of their mutual friend, A. R. Orage. Both Nott and Orage were students of Gurdjieff; although Saurat was not a student, he had met Gurdjieff and read *All and Everything*. Nott tells us that Saurat "began to talk about the Mortalists, a sect that Milton took a great interest in, whose descendants are the Christadelphians. According to the Mortalists when a man dies he is dead indeed. He sleeps as it were until the universe comes to an end; then, the universe is reborn and everything repeats. When a man's time comes, he is reborn." Nott writes,

> According to Gurdjieff—and to Milton and his Mortalists—not all men have souls, but there are those who consciously, or unconsciously, have acquired the germ of a soul, and this must be perfected.

This conversation between Saurat and Nott raises a number of questions. Is it possible that the seventeenth-century Puritan John Milton, author of *Paradise Lost*, taught that human beings are not born with a soul but must develop one? What did the religious sect known as the Mortalists believe about the soul, and what relationship did their beliefs have to Milton's? And is there a connection between John Milton and the Mortalists, and Gurdjieff's teaching on the soul?

John Milton

John Milton's epic poem *Paradise Lost* is often compared in importance to Homer's *Iliad* and Dante's *Divine Comedy*. Milton was a rebel, even a heretic, according to many theologians of his day. Milton's religious views informed his politics, and his politics informed his religious views. Zealously antipapist and antimonarchic, he was a loyal follower of Oliver Cromwell, the man who toppled the British monarchy during the seventeenth century, and he served in Cromwell's administration. Milton's opposition to both the English monarchy and the Church of England are recurring themes in his writings.

Milton was born on December 9, 1608. Highly educated, he wrote and spoke Latin, Greek and Italian. His biblical studies were aided by his capacity to read not just Hebrew, but also Aramaic and Syriac. He was privately tutored for years before attending the famous St. Paul's School. Milton also attended Christ's College, Cambridge, from 1625 until 1632, where he was a distinguished student and received his bachelor's and master's degrees.

Although his father expected him to enter the church, Milton studied at home for the next six years to become a poet, which he felt was his calling. A. W. Verity, in his biographical introduction to Milton's *Samson Agonistes*, writes, "It was Milton's constant resolve to achieve something that should vindicate the ways of God to men, something great that should justify his own possession of unique powers—powers of which, with no trace of egotism, he proclaims himself proudly conscious."

In 1641, Milton published his first prose work, *Of Reformation Touching Church-Discipline in England: And the Causes That Hitherto Have Hindered It*. Among the chief hindrances he cited was the role of the Church of England, which he saw as incompatible with civil liberty.

In 1642, at the age of thirty-four, Milton married seventeen-year-old Mary Powell. During their tumultuous marriage, Milton became blind in one eye and was greatly concerned that he might lose sight in the other one. Mary died in 1652, three days after the birth of their fourth child, who died a few days later. In 1656, now totally blind, he married Katherine Woodstock, with whom he found the love and the domestic society he craved. But she died two years later, three months after giving birth to their daughter, and the infant died five weeks after that. Milton married his third wife, Elizabeth Minshull, in 1662. She was twenty-four; he was fifty-four. Although this arrangement was intended to provide care for the blind Milton and his children, they developed considerable affection for each other.

With the restoration of the monarchy in 1660 and the return to the throne of King Charles II, Milton's political career had come to an end. The consequences of it, however, did not. He lived in fear of being executed by the regime of Charles II due to his antimonarchist writings. Although he was imprisoned for some weeks in 1660, he was never formally declared to be a traitor. Nevertheless, several of his closest friends were executed and others imprisoned during this period.

The rest of Milton's years were spent writing, outside the turmoil of politics. Milton had begun writing *Paradise Lost* in 1658; it was completed in 1665 and published in 1667. *Paradise Regained* and *Samson Agonistes* were published in 1671. In addition, Milton worked on *De Doctrina Christiana*, a prose text in which he formulates his fundamental ideas on God, religion, and the proper life, beginning in approximately 1658, and likely worked on it up to the time of his death in 1674. *De Doctrina* was not published, however, until 1825. These four works—*Paradise Lost, Paradise Regained, Samson Agonistes,* and *De Doctrina*—together spell out Milton's views on the soul, immortality, creation and the cosmos.

As we will see, Milton's beliefs had a significant impact on the teachings of the Mortalists in the seventeenth century and, as scholars have noted, on the works of Locke and Hobbes. While parallels may be drawn between Milton's beliefs and Gurdjieff's teaching of The Fourth Way, on the issue of the soul they do not appear to be as similar as C. S. Nott suggests.

Milton's Views on the Soul

Milton rejected the belief held by the Roman Catholic Church, the Church of England and many Protestant sects in an immaterial and immortal soul, one that exists separate and apart from the physical body. This teaching, based on Plato and the Neoplatonists, has been at the foundation of numerous orthodox Christian teachings from the time of the Augustine of Hippo in the fourth century, including the doctrine of original sin and the doctrines of heaven, hell and purgatory. Milton saw the church's teaching of the soul as an intentional misreading of the Bible, arguing at great length in *De Doctrina* that nowhere in the scripture can be found support for the proposition that man is born with an immortal soul that survives the body after death. For example, he says in *De Doctrina*,

> That the spirit of man should be separate from the body, so as to have a perfect and intelligent existence independently

of it, . . . is evidently at variance both with nature and reason . . . For the word *soul* [as used in scriptures] is applied to every kind of living being . . .

Nor has the word *spirit* any other meaning in the sacred writings, but that breath of life which we inspire, or the vital, or sensitive, or rational faculty, or some action or affection belonging to those faculties.

Without stating so explicitly, Milton bases his concept of the soul on Aristotelian theory—the body and soul are one and the same. In *De Doctrina*, Milton states,

> Man is a living being, intrinsically and properly one and individual, not compound or separable, not, according to the common opinion, made up and framed of two distinct and different natures, as of soul and body,—but that the whole man is soul, and the soul man, that is to say, a body, or substance individual, animated, sensitive and rational; and that the breath of life ["soul," as used in the Bible] was neither a part of the divine essence, nor the soul itself, but as it were an inspiration of some divine virtue fitted for the exercise of life and reason, and infused into the organic body; for man himself, the whole man, when finally created, is called in express terms a *living soul*. [Emphasis in original.]

Throughout his book *Milton: Man and Thinker*, Saurat reiterates that Milton does not believe in the existence of the soul. "Body and soul are for him one and the same thing. The word 'soul' is merely an abstract expression which separates arbitrarily the higher from the lower faculties and corresponds to no separate reality." And since the soul and the body are one, the soul perishes at death with the body. Milton says,

> For . . . what could be more absurd, than that the mind [soul], which is the part principally offending, should escape the threatened death; and that the body alone, to which immortality was equally allotted, before death came into the

world by sin, should pay the penalty of sin by undergoing death, though not implicated in the transgression?

For Milton, death is necessary as a result of sin. "The death of the body is to be considered in the light of a punishment for sin." Referring to Adam and Eve's fall from grace and banishment from the Garden of Eden, Milton says, "Therefore, that bodily death from which we are to rise again, originated in sin, and not in nature; contrary to the opinion of those who maintain that temporal death is the result of natural causes, and that eternal death alone is due to sin."

Milton's Materialism

A key element of Milton's cosmology and ontology (the nature of being) is that everything is *material* and that all matter is directly from God. In *De Doctrina*, Milton states, "God is the primary, and absolute, and sole cause of all things." Because "all things are of God," the original matter from which everything is made is part of God. Saurat tells us that "this is the fundamental doctrine of *Paradise Lost* and of the *Treatise of Christian Doctrine*, that the body is not only from, but of the Lord: the body is a part of God, matter is a part of the Divinity." And being created of God, the body, despite its physical death, "cannot finally be annihilated."

> God is neither willing, nor, properly speaking, able to annihilate anything altogether. He is not willing, because he does everything with a view to some end,—but nothing can be the end neither of God, nor of anything whatever... God is not able to annihilate anything altogether, because by creating nothing he would create and not create at the same time, which involves a contradiction.

Since everything existing is in its essence divine, "the covenant with God is not dissolved by death." In other words, even though there is no soul that can be separated from the body, because the body/spirit is made of divine matter and is therefore indestructible, every being is, as Saurat puts it, "naturally and normally immortal." Saurat summarizes,

"A key element in Milton is the idea of matter as good, imperishable and divine, a part of God himself from which all things issue spontaneously; so that there is no soul, and all beings are parts of God, arranged on an evolutionary scheme."

As can be seen, despite his dismissal of the traditional Christian view of the soul and his insistence that at death "a man had to die wholly," Milton believes deeply in immortality. And immortality is inextricably linked not only with Milton's materialism but also, just as importantly, with his teaching on the resurrection.

Milton, Immortality & the Resurrection

According to Milton, resurrection must take place because

> were there no resurrection, the righteous would be of all men most miserable, and the wicked who had a better position in this life, the most happy; which would be altogether inconsistent with the providence and justice of God.

Milton rejects any suggestion that there is an intermediate state between death and resurrection: "there are only two states, the mortal and the immortal, death and resurrection, not a word is said [in scripture] of any intermediate condition." Citing *The Gospel of John*, Milton declares in *De Doctrina* that, "there is not even a place appointed for the abode of the saints in heaven, till the resurrection." He tells us that even Saint Paul, whom Milton relies on extensively, must wait for his crown until "the same time when it was to be conferred on the rest of the saints, that is, not till the appearance of Christ in glory." Therefore, in direct contradiction of traditional theology, there is no purgatory, and heaven and hell will not exist until after the resurrection of the dead and the final judgment. For as Milton insists, there is "no recompense of good or bad after death, previous to the day of judgment."

At the resurrection, "every man will rise numerically one and the same person," having been "called out of the tomb." The resurrection will take place "on earth" and will be followed by the Last Judgment, at which "Christ, with the Saints, will judge the evil angels and the whole race of mankind." The "rule of judgment will be the conscience of each individual, according to the measure of light which he has enjoyed." Once sentence has been passed, it will be executed "by punishment of the wicked, and perfect glorification of the righteous." For the damned, the place of the punishment is hell, and punishment varies according to the degree of guilt. The punishment consists partly in

> the loss of the chief good, namely, the favour and protection of God, and the beatific vision of his presence, which is commonly called the punishment of loss; and partly in eternal torment, which is called the punishment of sense.

For the righteous, perfect glorification consists of eternal life and perfect happiness, arising chiefly from the divine vision.

As Saurat tells us, Milton believed that without this final glorification of the righteous and vengeance for the wicked, "the history of mankind would be too lamentable, and God too unjust; for as the wicked triumphed on the Earth, so retribution must take place on the Earth also."

Milton & the Mortalists

According to Saurat, "we come closest of all to Milton's most personal ideas in a group of his immediate contemporaries, the Mortalists." The Mortalists were a religious sect in seventeenth-century England who, like Milton, believed that (1) the body and soul are one, (2) there is no soul separate from the body that survives death, and (3) the resurrection of the body will occur at the end of time. The sect had its roots in the teachings of John Wycliffe, a dissident English priest and theologian in the 1300s who was the first person to translate the Bible into English. A century later, William Tyndale, a priest who became a leading figure in the Protestant Reformation, followed Wycliffe's beliefs in the mortality of the soul and the second coming of Christ at the final Day of Judgment. These dissident English theologians also believed, like Milton, that Christians should rely on the Bible as religious authority and not on the teachings of popes and clerics.

Although rejection of the immortality of the soul in England can be traced back to Wycliffe and Tyndale, it was not until Milton's time that a "systematic exposition of mortalist theory" was put into writing. In 1644, Richard Overton, a British printer and bookseller, published a small pamphlet entitled *Man's Mortality*, in which he spelled out the key tenets of the religion. In it, Saurat tells us, "We meet with arguments, quotations and expressions most familiar to us in Milton." The title page of Overton's pamphlet, *Man's Mortality*, serves as an executive summary of the Mortalists' beliefs:

> Mans mortallitie or a treatise Wherein 'tis proved, both Theologically and Phylosophically, that whole Man (as a rational! Creature) is a Compound wholly mortall, contrary to that common distinction of Soule and Body: And that the present going of the Soule into Heaven or Hell is a meer Fiction: And that at the Resurrection is the beginning of our immortallity, and then Actuall Condemnation, and Salvation, and not before.
>
> With Doubts and Objections answered and resolved, both by *Scripture* and *Reason*, discovering the multitude of *Blasphemies* and *Absurdities* that arise from the fancy of the *Soul*.

The pamphlet was published again in 1655 as *Man Wholly Mortal*. Saurat dedicated an entire chapter in his book *Milton: Man and Thinker* to proving that there was a relationship between Milton and this Mortalist sect during Milton's lifetime.

In the pamphlet, Overton attacks "the Hell-hatch'd doctrine of th'immortalle soule," arguing that it is a "distortion of the truth as it was originally revealed and recorded in Scripture, and a foundation for other false doctrinal assertions emanating from Rome, namely hell and purgatory." The pamphlet emphasizes that when a person dies, he or she ceases to exist:

> After death, "man is voyd of actuall Being", he absolutely IS NOT.
>
> ... man (not his flesh only, for that makes not man; but flesh and Spirit *sensu conjuncto* make Man) is not as a Tree, when

> He is cut down, whose Spirit liveth, and sprout|eth forth, and continueth: but as the flower of the field, (not the stalke, but the bare flower,) which totally fadeth and perisheth: Therefore Man is wholly mortal. [Emphasis in the original.]

Overton refers to "the ridiculous invention of the soul" and argues that nothing remains after death.

With reference to Christ's second coming, Overton says that believers will receive their "Crown of Righteousness . . . at that day," and therefore, "none ever entered into Heaven since Creation." This tracks what Milton said in *De Doctrina*: "Nay, Paul himself affirms that the Crown of Righteousness which was laid up for him was not to be received before that last day."

Saurat notes that "both [Milton and the Mortalists] come to the conclusion that God lets nature do her work and does not interfere, by creating a soul, at each birth." Instead, Overton reiterates what Saurat refers to as one of Milton's "noblest ideas"—that the soul is a part of what passes from parent to child at conception.

Saurat concludes that "Milton knew the pamphlet *Man's Mortality*, discussed it with the authors, who were among his friends, and absorbed the very substance of it." However, there was one significant difference between the first version of the *Man's Mortality* and Milton's own work, which Saurat emphasizes—in the entire pamphlet there are only a few references to the resurrection and the promised immortality after the Last Judgment. Significantly, the 1655 edition included eight new pages that address just that topic, and Saurat believes Milton was involved in drafting those passages.

In *Man Wholly Mortal*, the added references to the resurrection have the familiar ring of Milton himself: "That which is finite and mortal ceaseth from the time of the grave until the time of the resurrection." Likewise, the 1655 version tells us that at death man returns to what he was before birth—nothing, and will remain so until the resurrection:

> And so there is no more time to him after his death to the Resurrection, or recomposition of his elements, then there was to him from the creation to his birth, which is none at all.

> That which is not partly immortal as well as mortal [i.e., man], doth cease from life or Being from the time of the grave till the Resurrection.

And this resurrection occurs for all on the final day, at the second coming of Christ, not before—"the salvation of our souls, is . . . the day of judgment."

Regarding the origin of the soul, *Man Wholly Mortal* references the early theologians, Tertullian and Jerome, the Western Church, and Augustine to prove that the soul goes from father to son at generation because the soul is one with the body. This is an argument that Milton takes great pains to make in *De Doctrina*, quoting numerous passages from the Bible to support his theory. In *Man Wholly Mortal*, Overton quotes to precisely the same collection of authorities, in the same order as found in chapter seven of *De Doctrina*.

Thus, Saurat concludes that Milton was deeply involved in the revision of the pamphlet that was published as *Man Wholly Mortal* in 1655. According to Saurat, Milton's influence shifted the tone of the Mortalists' pamphlet and "lifted their whole conception into a more religious atmosphere. He gives to the second pamphlet the elevated tone that was somewhat lacking in the first," and "infused it with his own intensely religious spirit."

In his 2008 book *The Soul Sleepers*, Bryon Ball notes that John Milton, Thomas Hobbes and John Locke were "convinced mortalists." He goes on to say, "On account of the extent of their writings or their own prominence, they may be regarded as the major mortalist spokesmen of the seventeenth century . . . [whose influence] extended into the eighteenth century and even beyond." Thus, over eighty years after publishing *Milton: Man and Thinker* in 1925, Saurat's argument that John Milton was a Mortalist was vindicated.

Nott, Saurat & Gurdjieff's Teaching on the Soul

Having explored Milton's teaching on the soul and his relationship with the Mortalists, we return to the questions raised at the beginning of this essay. What does C. S. Nott's description of his conversation with Denis Saurat after the death of their friend Orage tell us about

Milton's and the Mortalists' views on the soul? Did Milton teach that human beings are not born with a soul but must develop one? What did Milton and the Mortalists believe about the soul and recurrence? Is there a connection between John Milton, the Mortalists and Gurdjieff's teaching on the soul?

It is helpful to place the conversation between Nott and Saurat, recounted in *Journey Through This World*, in its historical context. Saurat published his book, *Milton: Man and Thinker*, in 1925. He tells us in the preface to the book that parts one through three were written as his dissertation for his doctorate degree, which he received from the Sorbonne in 1920, published under the title *La pensée de Milton*. He expresses his frustration that, while the book was favorably reviewed, "the upper strata of the 'scholarly critics' refused to admit the originality of Milton's thought—without, however, suggesting any adequate sources" for the origin of those thoughts. It was actually Orage who put Saurat on the path to write part four of the book by suggesting that Milton "belonged to the same school" as William Blake, who was a kabbalist. Saurat later determined that Milton, too, drew much of his material from the Zohar, the main book of the Kabbalah. As a result, part four of *Milton: Man and Thinker* includes a section entitled "Contemporary Sources and Influences" and a chapter on "The Zohar and Kabbalah." The conversation between Nott and Saurat took place just weeks after Orage's death on November 6, 1934, nine years after Saurat published *Milton: Man and Thinker*. It is possible that Saurat changed his views dramatically between the time he published the book and the conversation recounted by Nott. However, there is nothing in Saurat's book, nor in a reading of Milton's work or the Mortalists' pamphlets, that suggests what Nott tells us as fact: that according to Gurdjieff and to Milton and the Mortalists, not all men have souls, but some have acquired a germ of a soul that they must perfect.

To the contrary, as Saurat established with great thoroughness in his book, both Milton and the Mortalists insisted that the body and soul are a unified whole, that at death this whole is extinguished and no longer exists, and that on the final Day of Judgment there will be a resurrection of the whole body/soul unity. Nowhere is the idea expounded that there is a germ of a *soul* that must be perfected.

In discussing the relationship between Milton's beliefs and the Zohar, Saurat tells us that while many of Milton's ideas can be found in the Zohar, "Milton evidently took only what suited him from that chaos of ideas," and what Milton took was only a very small part of the Zohar's contents. Saurat notes that "the most striking fact of all is that in the Zohar can be found all Milton's ideas . . . with one reservation only." That one reservation is Milton's "*idea of the non-existence of the soul.*" For in fact, a primary focus of the Zohar is the development of a separately existing soul over many lifetimes.

Bringing home the point, Saurat goes on to say, conversely, "there is only one great idea of the Zohar which is not in Milton: the idea of reincarnation." Nor, as we have seen, is there anything in Milton or the Mortalists suggesting the concept of recurrence. Yet Nott tells us that, according to Saurat, for the Mortalists (and by implication, Milton), at death, man "sleeps as it were until the Universe comes to an end; then the universe is reborn and everything repeats. When a man's time comes he is reborn." Nott goes on to quote Saurat,

> But . . . in the state of death our idea of time does not exist because time is the measure of motion (what Gurdjieff calls "the lawful fragmentation of some great whole") and in death there is no motion. Therefore, the interval between death and resurrection, however long it may seem to the living, does not exist for the dead; or at least, only as a night's sleep.

Nott then tells the reader that this is similar to Ouspensky's idea of recurrence. Perhaps that is what Saurat told him during their discussion. However, in the quote, Saurat uses the word *resurrection*—which, as we have seen, is a key term for Milton and the Mortalists. And the resurrection of which they speak occurs only once, at the second coming of Christ on the final Day of Judgment; it is entirely different from Ouspensky's idea that the same life is repeated again and again.

Nevertheless, there are connections that can be drawn between Gurdjieff's teachings and Milton's work. These will be explored below.

Milton's Esotericism

There is no reason to believe that Milton's views on immortality and the soul ever stagnated. It is abundantly clear that he was a man of great intellect who continued to question. One of his last works, *Paradise Regained*, completed ten years after the Mortalist tracts, clearly demonstrates that he was putting his most cherished values in question, including his views on the soul. While Milton may or may not have been steeped in authentic esoteric teachings, his writing suggests exposure to esoteric ideas, if not practices. Saurat, in *Milton: Man and Thinker*, describes aspects of a religion that is "peculiar to Milton." And despite Milton's rejection of the independent existence of the soul, in this religion to which Saurat refers, we can find certain parallels to The Fourth Way that Gurdjieff brought, whose origins are in esoteric Christianity.

Saurat tells us that according to Milton, after the Fall, which brought death into the world as well as Adam and Eve's expulsion from the Garden of Eden ("Paradise Lost"), a second creation was needed. It is this second creation that is integral to Saurat's description of a religion peculiar to Milton. God's first creation, the Son, is the source of all that is, the Creator God. After the Fall, from within the Son comes a second creation, Christ. And it is Christ who creates from within himself the Elect, in whom He is incarnated. As Saurat explains, "Christ is the Elect, the 'Greater Man,' the assembly of all men who alone deserve the name of 'man.'"

Christ's function has two aspects, one external, the promulgation of the divine truth; the other internal, the illumination of understanding. As Milton writes in *Paradise Regained*, God says of Christ,

> Men hereafter may discern
> From what consummate virtue I have chose
> This perfect man, by merit call'd my Son,
> To earn salvation for the sons of men.

A Higher Being Body

Through Christ, what Milton calls regeneration is possible. This is a change operated by the Word and the Spirit, whereby "the old [fallen] man being destroyed" leads to the emergence of a new man. That is, "the inward man is regenerated by God after His own image." Milton sometimes uses the phrase "born again" as synonymous with regeneration; he also describes the process as a being "created afresh" now of "incorruptible seed," for this is a birth of something new within the man. It is akin to the creation of a higher body within the physical body. Gurdjieff teaches that in esoteric Christianity the development of higher being-bodies is recognized as a possibility. Employing Christian terminology, Gurdjieff speaks of the natural body, the spiritual body and the divine body. In these higher being-bodies, he explains, "There is one single I, whole, indivisible, and permanent; there is individuality, dominating the physical body and its desires and able to overcome both its reluctance and its resistance." This man has consciousness and will. In like manner, Milton explains that by the phrase "God after His own image" he means a man who has regenerated "insomuch that he becomes as it were a new creature, and the whole man is sanctified both in body and soul, for the service of God, and the performance of good works." Such a man has free will and can exercise right judgment because he is infused "from above" with "new and supernatural faculties." Milton thus depicts what it means to be among the Elect, who are "planted in Christ."

Of course, for Milton, the Elect are those who believe in God:

> It is obvious therefore that God here divides the world into believers and unbelievers; and that in declaring, on the one hand, that *whosoever believeth in him shall not perish,* he implies on the other hand, as a necessary consequence, that whosoever believeth not, shall perish.

Despite this pronouncement, Milton asserts that Christ came to save all—not just the Elect but also those who are referred to as reprobates. This saving begins through God's calling. "This calling is either general or special. The general calling is that whereby God invites the whole of mankind, in various ways, but all of them sufficient for the purpose, to the knowledge of the true Deity." Milton further explains that "God's special calling is that whereby he, at the time which he thinks proper, invites particular individuals, elect as well as reprobate, more frequently, and with a more marked call than others." What happens as a result of being called? Milton says, "The natural mind and will of man being partially renewed by a divine impulse, are led to seek the knowledge of God, and for the time, at least, undergo an alteration for the better." This suggests a beginning that must be perpetuated—the divine impulse must be acted on to ensure salvation. Thus, Milton says that election alone does not assure salvation; one must also "continue to the end."

Regarding these efforts, Gurdjieff says, "Fusion, inner unity, is obtained by means of 'friction,' by the struggle between 'yes' and 'no' in man. If a man lives without inner struggle, if everything happens in him without opposition, if he goes wherever he is drawn or wherever the wind blows, he will remain such as he is. But if a struggle begins in him, and particularly if there is a definite line in this struggle, then, gradually, permanent traits begin to form themselves, he begins to 'crystallize.'"

According to Milton, with the hearing or harkening, we are temporarily given the power to act freely, a power that was lost with the Fall. This power of volition "cannot be wrought in us, without the power of free agency being at the same time imparted; since it is in this power that the will itself consists."

Saurat posits that because "Milton does not believe in the soul," Milton must mean that Christ is in the Elect materially, "probably in Milton's mind as a very sort of subtle material substance."

According to Saurat, however, it is more accurate to say that the Elect are in Christ, as He is the whole and they are the parts. In the same way that for Milton we are parts of Adam's substance inheriting the proclivity to sin, we can become regenerated through the substance of Christ and, through Christ, achieve eternal salvation.

The Three Temptations

Christ is the Greater Man because mankind can be regenerated in Him. So in *Paradise Regained*, when Satan is tempting Christ, he is tempting the whole of the new man. *Paradise Regained*, which is a retelling of the biblical account of Satan's three temptations of Christ, is Milton's message to all mankind that regeneration does not take place through any external power but through our own will. And the will through which this can be achieved is a fragment of God's will. That is, to be saved in Christ, we must participate in His merits. Aspects of these merits are demonstrated in Milton's poem.

Milton's temptations diverge in some significant ways from the biblical texts. In the biblical texts the three temptations are:

- Turn stones into bread to alleviate his own hunger; Jesus had been fasting in the desert for forty days.
- Worship the devil in return for all the kingdoms of the world.
- Jump from the highest point of a temple and rely on angels to break his fall.

In response, Jesus merely quotes scripture and declines three times.

Of course, Milton's employment of these temptations and Jesus's response in *Paradise Regained* is to be contrasted by the reader to what Milton depicts in *Paradise Lost*, when Adam and Eve are beguiled by Satan in the form of a serpent and, in disobedience to God's Word, succumb to the temptation and eat of the tree of knowledge, bringing death into the world. Jesus is the second Adam, the new man who will restore humanity through his obedience to God in the face of Satan's temptations. At the end of *Paradise Lost,* as the angel Michael is leading Adam and Eve from the Garden of Eden, he informs them that in time a savior will come who will defeat not Satan himself, but the effects of his deed. This will be accomplished through what Adam and Eve failed to do: obey the Word of God.

> Which he, who comes thy Saviour, shall recure,
> Not by destroying SATAN, but his works
> In thee and in thy Seed: nor can this be,
> But by fulfilling that which thou didst want,
> Obedience to the Law of God, impos'd.

In *Paradise Regained*, Satan believes that Jesus has been sent by God to destroy him; throughout the poem he refers to this in a literal way, and so is seeking to lead Jesus astray from his mission and to preserve his dominion over the earth. Milton's poem does not recreate the temptations as they appear in the biblical texts. After Jesus has been fasting in the desert for forty days, Satan appears to him disguised as a shepherd. Like the biblical text, Milton's first temptation is Satan's offer for Jesus to turn the stones into bread. But in *Paradise Regained*, Satan offers this not only so that Jesus can alleviate his own hunger but also as an act of charity to feed the people living in the surrounding area who are hungry. In his response, Jesus reveals that he knows who Satan really is and answers in words establishing that he is planted firmly in the spiritual world:

> Man lives not by Bread only, but each Word
> Proceeding from the mouth of God.

Jesus is thus indicating here that he will not submit to Satan's authority, only to the Word of God.

The second temptation takes up the bulk of the poem and is broken down into a number of temptations. Here is where Milton puts into question his own life, for Satan is offering to Jesus what Milton has been pursuing throughout his life: wealth, political power, the capacity to pursue classical wisdom, poetic eloquence and fame.

Of course, Jesus declines all temptations. In response to Satan's offer of the power to rule, Jesus does not quote scripture but points out the need to rule oneself and suggests parallels between the multitudes a king must rule and the multitudes within each of us:

> Yet he who reigns within himself, and rules
> Passions, Desires, and Fears, is more a King;
> Which every wise and vertuous man attains:
> And who attains not, ill aspires to rule
> Cities of men or head-strong Multitudes,
> Subject himself to Anarchy within,
> Or lawless passions in him which he serves.
> But to guide Nations in the way of truth
> By saving Doctrine, and from errour lead
> To know, and knowing worship God aright,
> Is yet more Kingly, this attracts the Soul,
> Governs the inner man, the nobler part.

To students of The Fourth Way, this will sound familiar. As we've seen, The Fourth Way teaches that we have no indivisible I; we are a bundle of "I"s. Gurdjieff tells us, "It is the greatest mistake to think that man is always one and the same. A man is never the same for long. He is continually changing. He seldom remains the same even for half an hour." Gurdjieff teaches that each "I" "does what it likes regardless of everything, and later on, the others have to pay for it. And there is no order among them whatever. Whoever gets the upper hand is master ... Imagine a country where everyone can be king for five minutes and do for these five minutes just what he likes with the whole kingdom. That is our life." For this reason, when Gurdjieff asks his students about their aims and receives their responses, he emphasizes that the best formulation is to be one's own master. Gurdjieff tells his students, "Without this, nothing else is possible." As Gurdjieff explains,

> For to be a Christian means to have the being of a Christian, that is, to live in accordance with Christ's precepts. Man number one, number two, and number three cannot live in accordance with Christ's precepts because with them everything 'happens.' Today it is one thing and tomorrow it is quite another thing. Today they are ready to give away their last shirt and tomorrow to tear a man to pieces because he refuses to give up his shirt to them. They are swayed by every chance event. They are not masters of themselves and therefore they cannot decide to be Christians and really be Christians.

The most telling aspect of Milton's self-reference in the second temptation is when Satan presents Athens to Jesus, offering him its great worldly wisdom and what Milton most cherishes as a poet—"Eloquence."

> Look once more e're we leave this specular Mount
> Westward, much nearer by Southwest, behold
> Where on the Ægean shore a City stands
> Built nobly, pure the air, and light the soil,
> *Athens* the eye of *Greece*, Mother of Arts
> and Eloquence, native to famous wits.

Satan attempts to lure Jesus with a variety of enticements: the wisdom of Plato and his academy, the poetry of Homer, schools of ancient sages who taught Alexander to subdue the world, Aristotle's Lyceum, the knowledge of the Epicureans and the Stoics, and even to "hear and learn the secret power of harmony in tones and numbers hit." Satan literally offers Jesus access to all the great texts, either from a library with the books available on a "revolving" basis or ownership of all the classics in his home. It is by acquiring the knowledge available through these sources that Jesus will, according to Satan, become complete as a ruler:

> These rules will render thee a King compleat
> Within thy self, much more with Empire joyn'd.

In response, Jesus simply states that this worldly knowledge has no value:

> Think not but that I know these things, or think
> I know them not; not therefore am I short
> Of knowing what I aught: he who receives
> Light from above, from the fountain of light,
> No other doctrine needs, though granted true;
> But these are false, or little else but dreams,
> Conjectures, fancies, built on nothing firm.

Jesus concludes with a reference to Socrates:

> The first and wisest of them all profess'd
> To know this only, that he nothing knew.

The aim of The Fourth Way is to acquire self-knowledge and ultimately Objective or Divine Reason. Gurdjieff's teaching also shows us that the path toward the wisdom and understanding of Socrates must take us from our egoistic beliefs about our own knowledge to the understanding that we know nothing. As Gurdjieff tells a perplexed student who said he used to think that he understood, but having been in the Work for some time, "now I do not understand anything." Gurdjieff says, "It means you have begun to understand. When you understood nothing, you thought you understood everything or at any rate that you were able to understand everything. Now, when you have begun to understand, you think you do not understand. This comes about because the *taste of understanding* was quite unknown to you before. And now the taste of understanding seems to you to be a lack of understanding."

In *All and Everything*, Beelzebub explains to his grandson what it means to be a learned being on earth and what it means to be a truly learned being. As to the learned beings on the earth, he says, "There on your planet, the more of such information one of your favorites mechanically learns by rote, information he himself has never verified, and which moreover he has never sensed, the more learned he is considered to be." Truly learned beings, by contrast, are those who "acquire by their conscious labors and intentional sufferings the ability to contemplate the details of all that exists from the point of view of World-arising and World-existence, owing chiefly to which, they perfect their highest body to the corresponding gradation of the sacred measure of Objective Reason in order that they might later sense as much about cosmic truths as their higher being-body is perfected."

In *Paradise Regained*, the night before the third temptation, a truly hellish storm disturbs Jesus's sleep. One possibility for this storm in Milton's poem is to impress Jesus with Satan's power "as prince of an indifferent and mindless order of nature, to suggest that his Father has either forsaken him or is unable to reach him in a fallen world." That morning, Satan will again tempt Jesus. But Jesus's refusal of the first two temptations puts him far above other men, so Satan first raises questions of identity—needing to know why Jesus has been named the Son of God. He says,

> [I want to] learn
> In what degree or meaning thou art call'd
> The Son of God, which bears no single sense;
> The Son of God I also am, or was,
> And, if I was, I am; relation stands . . .

Satan is raising the issue of self-knowledge, expressing uncertainty about his own identity, and seeking to understand who Jesus thinks he is. And while it is clearly a ploy to set up the final temptation, the question remains.

Satan whisks Jesus up to the heights of the Temple of Jerusalem, placing him on its highest pinnacle, and there quotes the Psalms to show that Jesus can trust in the support of angels:

> Cast thy self down; safely if Son of God:
> For it is written, He will give command
> Concerning thee to his Angels, in thir hands
> They shall up lift thee, lest at any time
> Thou chance to dash thy foot against a stone.

Jesus's answer as the concluding chord of the temptation is both ambiguous and profound. In rejecting this temptation, Jesus demonstrates that he knows who he is and why he was sent to the earth. He is obedient to God's Will, and because of that, in response he merely quotes scripture: "Also it is written, 'Tempt not the Lord thy God', he said and stood." With this terse response, Satan is vanquished.

Why is this so effective?

On the literal level, Jesus is simply saying that Satan should not put the Father to unnecessary tests. But what is Milton saying to his readers? One view has it that Jesus is showing us that we can exercise divine will:

> For Milton what man can do for himself is negative and iconoclastic: man does not save himself, but, by clearing his world of idols, he can indicate his willingness to be saved. Christ has resisted the whole of Satan's world; he has done what man can do . . . Thus, the fact that Christ successfully stands on the pinnacle is miraculous, but not a miracle drawn from his own divine nature . . . It means that his human will has been taken over by the omnipotent divine will at the necessary point and prefigures the commending of his spirit to the Father at the instant of his death on the cross.

But is there possibly more here? Is Milton suggesting that Jesus is saying that *he is* the Lord thy God? By quoting the Father's scripture, by adhering to his Father's will, Jesus is rewarded in his obedience with the knowledge that He is not only the Savior but is also in some sense God himself. Does this mean that Milton's religious beliefs encompass the possibility that by fulfilling our duty to God, we may experience unity with God or, as Gurdjieff says, Divine Reason? Did Milton come to believe that human beings can develop an immortal soul?

ENDNOTES

INTRODUCTION

1. *While secularism.* Phil Zuckerman, *Living the Secular Life: New Answers to Old Questions* (New York: Penguin Books, 2014), 2.
2. *What do you expect.* W. Somerset Maugham, *The Razor's Edge* (New York: Doubleday, Doran, 1944), 54.
3. *He had a thought.* Mark Oppenheimer, "The Evangelical Scion Who Stopped Believing," *New York Times Magazine*, December 29, 2016, https.//nyti.ms/2iHEtK9.
4. *What is the sense.* William Patrick Patterson, *The Life & Significance of George Ivanovitch Gurdjieff—Part I Gurdjieff In Egypt, The Origin of Esoteric Knowledge,* DVD (Fairfax, CA: Arete Communications, 2000). In *Gurdjieff in Egypt*, Patterson traces Gurdjieff's journey to Egypt in search of the origins of the esoteric teaching Gurdjieff later brought to the West as The Fourth Way.

CHAPTER ONE

THE FOURTH WAY

5. *Man in his history.* William Patrick Patterson, *Ladies of the Rope: Gurdjieff's Special Left Bank Women's Group* (Fairfax, CA: Arete Communications, 1999), 96.
6. *The representative of God.* Patterson, *Georgi Ivanovitch Gurdjieff: The Man, The Teaching, His Mission* (Fairfax, CA: Arete Communications, 2014), 142.

7. *Completely self-supporting.* P. D. Ouspensky, *In Search of the Miraculous* (New York: Harcourt, Brace and World, 1949), 286.
8. *A mathematical and material explanation.* Margaret Anderson, *The Unknowable Gurdjieff* (London: Arkana, 1991), 49.
9. *Only by understanding.* Ouspensky, *Search*, 40.
10. *Future machines will.* Ray Kurzweil, *The Singularity Is Near* (New York: Viking, 2005), 30.
11. *If a man is changing.* Ouspensky, *Search*, 101.
12. *Who is now one.* Ouspensky, *Search*, 31.
13. *To recognize that.* William Patrick Patterson, *Introduction to Gurdjieff's Fourth Way: From Selves to Individual Self to The Self* (Fairfax, CA: Arete Communications, 2012), DVD.
14. *Gurdjieff stressed the need.* Teresa Adams, "Gurdjieff and Pythagoras—The Hyperborean Apollo, Part II," *The Gurdjieff Journal*, Vol. 18, No. 2, p. 4.
15. *To have consciousness.* William Patrick Patterson, *Spiritual Survival in a Radically Changing World-Time* (Fairfax, CA: Arete Communications, 2009), 12–13.
16. *Once embodied, self-observation.* Patterson, *Spiritual Survival*, 13.
17. *Teaching extends.* Patterson, *Spiritual Survival*, 368.
18. *The whole secret.* Ouspensky, *Search*, 101–102.
19. *There are four ways.* Patterson, *Gurdjieff: The Man, The Teaching, His Mission*, 311.
20. *A blind man.* Ouspensky, *Search*, 195.
21. *Gurdjieff explains.* Ouspensky, *Search*, 40.
22. *The consciousness manifested.* Ouspensky, *Search*, 41.
23. *A man without.* Ouspensky, *Search*, 41.
24. *It is dust.* Ouspensky, *Search*, 94.
25. *In order to speak.* Ouspensky, *Search*, 31.
26. *What may be called.* Ouspensky, *Search*, 32.
27. *But the powders.* Ouspensky, *Search*, 43.
28. *In the sphere of the emotions.* Ouspensky, *Search*, 155.
29. *Conscience is a state.* Ouspensky, *Search*, 155.
30. *Conscience is the fire.* Ouspensky, *Search*, 156.
31. *From this crystallization.* Ouspensky, *Search*, 180.
32. *This is the transmutation.* Ouspensky, *Search*, 256.
33. *Has begun to accumulate.* G. I. Gurdjieff, *Views from the Real World: Early Talks of Gurdjieff* (New York: Dutton, 1973), 215.

34. *If it is not re-born.* And yet, years later in *All and Everything*, Gurdjieff writes that the astral body "must inevitably languish also forever in all kinds of exterior planetary forms." G. I. Gurdjieff, *All and Everything* (Aurora, OR: Two Rivers Press, 1993), 674.
35. *They are more correctly.* Ouspensky, *Search*, 197.
36. *The fourth body.* Ouspensky, *Search*, 93–94.
37. *Is his own knowledge.* Ouspensky, *Search*, 73.
38. *The Kesdjan body.* Gurdjieff, *All and Everything*, 766.
39. *Instantly enter this other.* Gurdjieff, *All and Everything*, 766.
40. *Okipkhalevnian-exchange.* Gurdjieff, *All and Everything*, 767.
41. *Because the soul is composed.* Gurdjieff, *All and Everything*, 768.
42. *An independent individual.* Gurdjieff, *All and Everything*, 765.
43. *Can, by the conscious and intentional.* Gurdjieff, *All and Everything*, 145.
44. *If we have some crystals.* Gurdjieff, *Views from the Real World*, 215.
45. *Man is an image.* Ouspensky, *Search*, 75.
46. *To the smallest detail.* Gurdjieff, *All and Everything*, 775.
47. *Arising and maintenance.* Gurdjieff, *All and Everything*, 137.
48. *Devoted Himself entirely.* Gurdjieff, *All and Everything*, 749–50. Apparently, the Creator God could not simply will away the effects of time on the Sun Absolute.
49. *Hence, if there is no conscious work.* Patterson, *Spiritual Survival*, 362–69.
50. *If the process [Djartklom] is conscience.* Adams, 11.
51. *Are all those separate functionings.* Gurdjieff, *All and Everything*, 775.
52. *The center of gravity.* William Patrick Patterson, *Voices in the Dark* (Fairfax, CA: Arete Communications, 2000), 93.
53. *The degree of one's consciousness.* Gurdjieff, *All and Everything*, 770.
54. *The Fourth Way.* Patterson, *Spiritual Survival*, 29.
55. *By engaging.* Patterson, *Spiritual Survival*, 29.

CHAPTER TWO

ANCIENT EGYPT

56. *The Universe is nothing.* R. A. Schwaller de Lubicz, *The Temple of Man* (Rochester, VT: Inner Traditions, 1998), 31. (When *De Lubicz* is used in a footnote, it refers to R. A. Schwaller De Lubicz.

All citations to books written by his wife, Isha, will be referenced with her full name, Isha Schwaller de Lubicz.)

57. *In Gurdjieff's quest.* Gurdjieff likely arrived in Egypt in 1895, although if the events recounted in *Meetings with Remarkable Men* are arranged chronologically, an alternative date of 1893 is possible. See *The Gurdjieff Journal*, Vol. 6, No. 1, p. 3.

58. *Gurdjieff was initiated.* Patterson, *Gurdjieff: The Man, The Teaching, His Mission*, 291.

59. *Obey our reductionist tendency.* R. A. Schwaller De Lubicz, *The Temple in Man* (Brookline, MA: Autumn Press, 1977), 18. De Lubicz traveled to Egypt in 1936 and stayed for 15 years, spending most of his time in Luxor (ancient Thebes). Out of his meticulous study of the ancient structures his two most remarkable books, *The Temple of Man* and *The Temples of Karnak*, were published. He began his writing in 1949 with a short book called *The Temple in Man*.

60. *Reality reveals itself.* De Lubicz, *The Temple of Man*, 2.

61. *Thus, the Egyptian mentality was indirect.* De Lubicz, *The Temple in Man*, 111.

62. *De Lubicz, recognizing that we.* De Lubicz, *The Temples of Karnak* (Rochester, VT: Inner Traditions, 1999), 7.

63. *The employment of forms.* De Lubicz, *The Temple of Man*, 22.

64. *The word de Lubicz preferred.* De Lubicz, *The Temple of Man*, xxvii & 21.

65. *Thus de Lubicz's use.* De Lubicz, *Sacred Science*, 120.

66. *It is the gesture.* De Lubicz, *Temple of Man*, 22

67. *Thus one's level.* De Lubicz, *Temple of Man*, 52, 57.

68. *Not the beginnings of research.* De Lubicz, *Temple in Man*, 20.

69. *That knowledge reveals.* De Lubicz, *Temple of Man*, 74. Isha Schwaller de Lubicz writes in *Her-Bak: Egyptian Initiate*, 24: "The problem of life is not yet fathomed, but the possibility of a Mother-who-dies-not brings you nearer a solution, for she reveals the meaning of death, which is no more than a passing of the creature into the belly of the great mother Nut who brings about all changes."

70. *Through its figurations.* De Lubicz, *Sacred Science*, 199.

71. *There has never.* De Lubicz, *Sacred Science*, 16.

72. *The error of our world.* R. A. Schwaller De Lubicz, *Nature Word* (West Stockbridge, MA: Lindisfarne Press, 1982), 71.
73. *The ancient name for Egypt.* De Lubicz, *The Temple in Man*, 12. The word *alchemy* derives from an Egyptian word *chem* or *qem*, meaning "black," referring to the black alluvial soils bordering the Nile. Nevill Drury, *Magic and Witchcraft* (London: Thames and Hudson, 2003), p. xx.
74. *We have nothing.* De Lubicz, *The Temple of Man*, 4.
75. *The inevitable resurrection.* De Lubicz, *The Temple in Man*, 12, from the translator's foreword by Robert Lawlor.
76. *The birth of divine man.* De Lubicz, *The Temple in Man*, 12, from the translator's foreword by Robert Lawlor.
77. *Thus through spiritual metabolism.* De Lubicz, *The Temple in Man*, 47.
78. *The body itself becomes energy.* De Lubicz, *The Temple in Man*, 45.
79. *According to the Papyrus of Turin.* M. Broderick and A. A. Morton, *A Concise Dictionary of Egyptian Archaeology* (London: Metheun & Co., 1903), 72–73. *See also* de Lubicz, *Sacred Science*, 86 & 111. By way of comparison, the Roman Empire lasted for less than 1,000 years. Today, Japan is the longest running existing empire. It has existed for 1,743 years from the start of its first historical emperor's reign or over 2,600 years if legendary emperors are considered. http://www.eupedia.com/forum/threads/28700-Longest-lived-empires-states-in-history.
80. *The striving to become aware.* Gurdjieff, *All and Everything*, 297.
81. *The Alkhaldans, however.* Gurdjieff, *All and Everything*, 301.
82. *The incursion of new people.* W. B. Emery, Archaic Egypt (London: Penguin, 1961), 38–39.
83. *Man, know thyself.* De Lubicz, *The Temples of Karnak*, 23.
84. *This thought has.* De Lubicz, *The Temples of Karnak*, 23.
85. *It is not a participant.* De Lubicz, *The Temples of Karnak*, 35.
86. *While the neters.* De Lubicz, *The Temples of Karnak*, 35.
87. *On our level.* Isha Schwaller de Lubicz, *Her-Bak: Egyptian Initiate*, 190.
88. *This awareness.* Isha Schwaller de Lubicz, *Her-Bak: Egyptian Initiate*, 193.
89. *As Horus grew.* Patterson, *Gurdjieff in Egypt*, DVD.

90. *Patterson explains.* Patterson, *Spiritual Pilgrimage: Mr. Gurdjieff's Father's Grave* (Fairfax, CA: Arete Communications), DVD, 2015.
91. *But Horus cannot.* Patterson, *Gurdjieff in Egypt*, DVD.
92. *Set becomes Horus's companion.* Patterson, *Gurdjieff in Egypt*, DVD.
93. *Horus enters.* Isha Schwaller de Lubicz, *Her-Bak: Egyptian Initiate*, 326–27.
94. *The purpose of this existence.* "Invariable truth is the equating of Consciousness with Being." De Lubicz, *The Temple of Man*, 28.
95. *She who sees.* Henri Frankfort, *Kingship and the Gods: A Study of Ancient Near Eastern Religion as the Integration of Society and Nature* (Chicago: University of Chicago Press, 1978), 21.
96. *For the masses.* De Lubicz, *The Temple of Man*, 9.
97. *Wheel of exhaustion.* De Lubicz, *The Temple of Man*, 9.
98. *This may lead.* De Lubicz, *The Temple of Man*, 9.
99. *The first stage.* Isha Schwaller de Lubicz, *Her-Bak: Egyptian Initiate*, 185.
100. *Thus, creation is a process.* The passage of the spiritual world into the corporal world is the mystery of incarnation. Isha Schwaller de Lubicz, *Her-Bak: Egyptian Initiate*, 188.
101. *The initial creative act.* Lucie Lamy, *Egyptian Mysteries* (New York: Crossroad, 1981), 8. Lucy Lamy is de Lubicz's daughter.
102. *This word serves.* De Lubicz, *The Temples of Karnak*, 29.
103. *Ra symbolizes.* Isha Schwaller de Lubicz, *Her-Bak: Egyptian Initiate*, 349.
104. *Those who reunite.* Isha Schwaller de Lubicz, *Her-Bak: Egyptian Initiate*, 191.
105. *The heat of his activity.* Isha Schwaller de Lubicz, *Her-Bak: Egyptian Initiate*, 184.
106. *Yet from duality.* Isha Schwaller de Lubicz, *Her-Bak: Egyptian Initiate*, 180.
107. *The Ancient Egyptians.* Bika Reed, *Rebel in the Soul* (Rochester, VT: Inner Traditions, 1997), 110.
108. *Ba is the second.* Isha Schwaller de Lubicz, *Her-Bak: Egyptian Initiate*, 193.
109. *Both Ba and Ka.* Isha Schwaller de Lubicz, *Her-Bak: Egyptian Initiate*, 193.
110. *It is hard to distinguish.* Isha Schwaller de Lubicz, *The Opening of the Way*, 204.

111. *Thus, Ba in relation.* Isha Schwaller de Lubicz, *The Opening of the Way*, 201.
112. *Although the function*, Reed, *Rebel in the Soul*, 108.
113. *The human soul.* Isha Schwaller de Lubicz, *Her-Bak: Egyptian Initiate*, 172, 175, 178 & 225.
114. *Struggle on the part.* Isha Schwaller de Lubicz, *Her-Bak: Egyptian Initiate*, 195.
115. *Mass of impure.* Isha Schwaller de Lubicz, *Her-Bak: Egyptian Initiate*, 193.
116. *The Me's desire.* Isha Schwaller de Lubicz, *Her-Bak: Egyptian Initiate*, 193.
117. *Divine, incorruptible, immortal.* Isha Schwaller de Lubicz, *Her-Bak: Egyptian Initiate*, 194.
118. *Signatures and the innate.* Isha Schwaller de Lubicz, *Her-Bak: Egyptian Initiate*, 362.
119. *The higher Ka.* Isha Schwaller de Lubicz, *Her-Bak: Egyptian Initiate*, 362.
120. *The difference in those.* Gurdjieff, *All and Everything*, 1001–02.

CHAPTER THREE

CHRISTIANITY

121. *The many forms.* Christianity is the largest religion in the modern world, approaching almost a third of the global population in the early twenty-first century. See *A Report on the Size and Distribution of the World's Christian Population*, Pew Research Center Religion & Public Life Project, http://www.pewforum.org/2011/12/19/global-christianity-exec/.
122. *Modern Biblical historians.* James D. Tabor, *Paul and Jesus: How the Apostle Transformed Christianity* (New York: Simon & Schuster, Inc., 2012), 71.
123. *And while the order.* For example, the Catholic Church dates the Gospel of Matthew at around 80 CE, fifty years after the death of Christ. David M. Stanley, S. J., *The Gospel of St. Matthew* (Collegeville, MN: The Liturgical Press, 1967), 5.
124. *The first reference.* Tabor, 72. Tabor dates the gospel of Mark at 80 CE, and the Gospel of Matthew at least ten years later.

125. *Do not fear those.* Matt 10:28. Unless otherwise noted, all citations are to the *New American Standard Bible*, Lockwood Foundation (La Habra, CA: Foundation Press, 1997).
126. *For what will it profit.* Matt. 16:26–27.
127. *Modern translations of this.* Numerous translations of Matt. 16:26–27 can be compared at http://biblehub.com/matthew/16-26.htm. See also Mark 8:36–37 and Luke 9:25 in various translations at the same website, http://biblehub.com.
128. *Behold, my servant.* Matt. 12:18. Some translations replace "in whom my soul is well-pleased" with variations on "in whom I am pleased." See http://biblehub.com/matthew/ 12–18.htm.
129. *Come to me.* Matt. 11:28–30.
130. *You shall love.* Matt. 22:37.
131. *In Mark the words.* Mark 12:30.
132. *What shall I do?* Luke 10:25–28.
133. *My soul exalts.* Luke 1:46–47.
134. *I will say to my soul.* Luke 12:19–20.
135. *My soul is deeply grieved.* Matt. 26:38–39, Mark 14:34–36.
136. *Now my soul is troubled.* John 12:27.
137. *Only about eight percent.* Floyd V. Filson, "*The Literary Relations among the Gospels,*" in Charles M. Laymon, ed., *The Interpreter's One-Volume Commentary on the Bible* (Nashville, TN: Abingdon Pres, 1991), 989.
138. *Instead, it begins with.* John 1:1–14.
139. *For God so loved.* John 3:16. Similar statements can be found in John 3:36, 6:40, and 11:25.
140. *Truly, truly, I say.* John 5:24.
141. *I am the living bread.* John 6:51.
142. *I am the resurrection.* John 11:25–26.
143. *Do not marvel.* John 5:28–29.
144. *For in the resurrection.* Matt. 22:30, Mark 12:25.
145. *And he was saying.* Luke 23:42–43.
146. *Paul wrote.* The first list identifying the twenty-seven books of the New Testament was written by Athanasius, bishop of Alexandria, in 367 CE, although not all were in agreement. Bruce Metzger, *The Canon of the New Testament: Its Origin, Development and Significance* (New York, Oxford University Press, 3rd ed., 1989), 7–8.

147. *Yet Paul's thirteen letters.* Thirteen of the New Testament's twenty-seven documents are Paul's letters (or those purporting to be written by him), and a fourteenth, the Acts of the Apostles, is predominantly the story of Paul's missionary work. Tabor, 227.
148. *Some scholars have gone.* Tabor, 6.
149. *For example, Tabor argues.* Tabor, xviii.
150. *Paraphrasing Alfred.* Alfred North Whitehead, *Process and Reality* (New York: Simon & Schuster, The Free Press, 1979), 39.
151. *It has often been said.* William Platcher and Derek Nelson, *A History of Christian Theology: An Introduction* (Louisville, KY: Westminster John Knox Press, 2nd ed., 2013), 21. Quoting Sydney Ahlstrom, "Christian theology is a series of footnotes to St. Paul."
152. *According to the Acts.* Acts 9:11.
153. *As Paul states.* Gal. 1:13, Phil. 3:5.
154. *This ended when.* Acts 1:1–9.
155. *Despite evidence.* Tabor, 6.
156. *There is also a question. See,* Hyam Maccoby, *The Mythmaker: Paul and the Invention of Christianity* (New York: Harper & Row, 1986).
157. *For I would have.* Gal. 1:11–12.
158. *Paul asserts.* Gal. 1:15–17. "But when God, who had set me apart even from my mother's womb and called me through His grace, was pleased to reveal His Son in me so that I might preach Him among the Gentiles, I did not immediately consult with flesh and blood, nor did I go up to Jerusalem to those who were apostles before me; but I went away to Arabia, and returned once more to Damascus."
159. *He considers himself.* 2 Cor. 11:5.
160. *Having worked harder.* 2 Cor. 11:23.
161. *Even though we have known.* 2 Cor. 5:16.
162. *Paul teaches.* 1 Cor. 15:29.
163. *And the resurrection.* Alan F. Segal, *Life After Death: A History of the Afterlife in the Religions of the West* (New York: Doubleday, 2004), 439.
164. *For as Segal notes.* Segal, 425.
165. *Boasting is necessary.* 2 Cor. 12:1–5.
166. *Instead, Paul states.* Segal, 411.
167. *Rather than arguing.* Segal, 430.

168. *This is the totality.* Segal, 429. Segal notes that although *soma psychikon* could mean the natural body in the Greek, it is not the most obvious term for it.
169. *And so the new body.* Segal, 429–30.
170. *Behold, I tell you.* 1 Cor. 15:51–57.
171. *For we know that.* 2 Cor. 5:1–3. *New Living Version Bible* translation.
172. *Paul always expected.* Tabor, 115.
173. *But because of your.* Rom. 2: 5–10.
174. *For we must all.* 2 Cor. 5:10.
175. *For the wages.* Rom. 6: 23.
176. *For you are all.* Gal. 3: 26–28.
177. *What the Gospels.* Segal, 439.

CHAPTER FOUR

AUGUSTINE AND AQUINAS: DEVELOPING THE TRADITIONAL CHRISTIAN THEORY OF THE SOUL

178. *The importance of Augustine's.* Elaine Pagels, *Adam, Eve, and the Serpent* (New York: Vintage Books, 1989), 98–126. In chapter five, "The Politics of Paradise," Pagels argues convincingly that the influence of Augustine throughout western Christianity has surpassed that of any other church father, primarily because his teachings on original sin and the nonexistence of free will laid the groundwork for the Catholic Church's alliance with imperial powers. Pagels, 126.
179. *Although the Roman.* Bart Ehrman and Andrew Jacobs, ed., *Christianity in Late Antiquity, 300–450 C.E.: A Reader* (New York: Oxford University Press, Inc., 2004), 4–5.
180. *In order to maintain.* Segal, 486–90.
181. *Love and seek and pursue.* Henry Chadwick, trans., *Saint Augustine: Confessions* (New York: Oxford University Press, 1998), 39 (III. iv. 8).
182. *According to its founder.* Samuel C. Lieu, *Manichaeism in the Later Roman Empire and Medieval China: A Historical Survey* (Oxford, England: Manchester University Press, 1985), 8. The founder of Manichaeism referred to himself as "the Apostle of Jesus Christ."

Richard C. Foltz, *Religions of the Silk Road* (New York: St. Martins Press, 1999), 75, but denied the historical reality of the crucifixion of Jesus. Chadwick, Introduction, xiv.

183. *Augustine later wrote.* Augustine was adamant that the soul was both created by God (as opposed to a substance of God per Manichaeism) and immaterial. Michael Mendelson, "Saint Augustine," *Stanford Encyclopedia of Philosophy* (Winter 2012 Edition), Edward N. Zalta (ed.). http://plato.stanford.edu/archives/win2012/entries /augustine/, 7.

184. *During his lifetime.* Mendelson, 2.

185. *Two of Augustine's works.* Etienne Gilson, "Introduction," *St. Augustine: City of God*, Gerald Walsh, et al., trans. (Garden City, NY: Doubleday, Image Books, 1958), 13.

186. *But, as described in Confessions.* Augustine, *Confessions*, 121–23 (VII.ix.13–15).

187. *Although Augustine's views.* Mendelson, 10.

188. *That is, a human being.* Augustine, *City of God*, 434–36 (XIX.3).

189. *Rational soul using.* Markus, 200, citing Augustine, *Of the Morals of the Catholic Church and On the Morals of the Manichaen*, (I.27.52).

190. *For Augustine, the death.* Bruno Niederbacher, "The Human Soul: Augustine's case for soul-body dualism," *The Cambridge Companion to Augustine*, David Merconi and Eleanor Stump, eds. (Cambridge, UK: Cambridge University Press, 2014), 127.

191. *After death.* Augustine, *Confessions*, 110 (VI.xvi.26).

192. *The deity would not.* Augustine, *Confessions*, 105 (VI.xi.19).

193. *Likewise, in Soliloquies.* Neiderbacher, 127.

194. *With avid intensity.* Augustine, *Confessions*, 130–31(VII.xxi.27).

195. *Who will deliver him.* Augustine, *Confessions*, 131 (VII.xxi.27), citing Paul in Romans 7:24.

196. *The heavenly body.* Segal, 580.

197. *As Segal explains.* Segal, 582.

198. *He notes that Augustine.* Segal, 580–81.

199. *The decline of Rome.* Markus, 206.

200. *As Elaine Pagels.* Pagels, 107.

201. *The desire to master.* Pagels, 107.

202. *The whole human race.* Pagels, 109.

203. *What epitomizes.* Pagels, 110–11.

204. *Humankind has.* Pagels, 113.

205. *Since Christians cannot.* Pagels, 117.
206. *Pagels argues.* Pagels, 126.
207. *Due to the universal contagion.* Mendelson, 20.
208. *Augustine clearly believes.* Neiderbacher, 128.
209. *Augustine states.* Neiderbacher, 128.
210. *Likewise, he posits.* Augustine, *City of God*, XXII.2.
211. *Although it be true.* Augustine, *City of God*, XXII.3.
212. *In contrast.* Segal, 581.
213. *Both infinitely superior.* Segal, 580.
214. *Augustine developed five.* Mendelson, 7–9.
215. *In Augustine's Letter 166.* Mendelson, 8.
216. *God created.* Mendelson, 8.
217. *Later in life.* Mendelson, 8–9, citing to Augustine, *The Soul and its Origins* 10.15.27.
218. *He also suggested a new theory.* Mendelson, 9, citing *City of God* XIII.14.
219. *This theory supported.* Augustine, *On the Soul and Origins* I.10, trans. in *Nicene and Post-Nicene Fathers*, Series I, Vol. V, http://www.ccel.org/fathers2/NPNF1-05-31.html.
220. *Near the end.* Mary Bogen, R.S.M, trans., *The Fathers of the Church: Augustine, The Retractations* (Washington DC: Catholic University Press, 1999), 28–31 (I.vii.2).
221. *Despite pressure.* Mendelson, 9. Augustine died on August 28, 430 CE, as the Vandals were laying siege to his city of Hippo.
222. *It has frequently.* Ralph McInerny and John O'Callaghan, "Saint Thomas Aquinas," *Stanford Encyclopedia of Philosophy* (Winter 2012 Edition), Edward N. Zalta, ed., 10. http://plato.stanford.edu/archives/win2012/entries/augustine/.
223. *Historian David Knowles.* David Knowles, *The Evolution of Medieval Thought* (New York: Random House, 1998), chapters 13–23.
224. *While controversial.* Pope Leo XIII, *Aeterni Patris: Encyclical of Pope Leo XIII on the Restoration of Christian Philosophy* (Rome: Libreria Editric Vaticana), No. 3, http://w2.vatican.va/content/leo-xiii/en/encyclicals/documents/hf_l-xiii_enc_ 04081879 _aeterni-patris.html.
225. *During Aquinas' lifetime.* Ralph McInerny, *Aquinas* (Cambridge, UK: Polity Press & Blackwell Publishing, Ltd., 2004), 4.

226. *Aquinas was born.* McInerny and O'Callaghan, 2.
227. *Frederick II.* G. K. Chesterson, *St. Thomas Aquinas* (New York: Sheed & Ward, 1933), 25.
228. *Thomas was the youngest.* Denys Turner, *Thomas Aquinas: A Portrait* (New Haven, CT: Yale University Press, 2013), 9.
229. *When he was only.* Turner, 9–10. As Turner describes it, "Monte Cassino, the first of Benedict's own foundations established in 529, was in the Ivy League of medieval monastic communities."
230. *Then, in April.* McInerny, 11.
231. *Appalled, his mother.* Chesterson, 33–34.
232. *Thomas snatched.* McInerny, 12.
233. *A huge bull.* Chesterson, 2.
234. *From there, Aquinas.* McInerny, 13–15.
235. *Aquinas' masterpiece.* Etienne Gilson, *The Spirit of Medieval Philosophy, Gifford Lectures 1933-35* (Notre Dame, IN: University of Notre Dame Press, 1991), 490.
236. *The first principle.* Aquinas, *Summa Theologica* I, Ques. 75, Art. 1, Fathers of the English Dominican Province, trans. (New York: Benziger Bros., 1947). Throughout the *Summa Theologica*, Aquinas contrasts the teachings of Augustine with his own positions and those of Aristotle.
237. *According to Aquinas.* Aquinas, *Summa Theologica* I Ques.75, Art. 4; Ques. 90, Art. 4.
238. *The body is.* Aquinas, *Summa Theologica* I, Ques. 76, Art. 1.
239. *For Aquinas.* Aquinas, *Summa Theologica* I, Ques. 90, Art. 4.
240. *In other words.* Turner, 71.
241. *Emphatically he denies.* Turner, 56.
242. *Like Aristotle.* Aquinas, *Summa Theologica* I, Ques. 76, Art. 3.
243. *For Aquinas.* Turner, 66.
244. *Instead, he asserts.* Aquinas, *Summa Theologica* I, Ques. 76, Art. 3.
245. *Human beings have one.* Turner, 69.
246. *Aquinas' theory of the soul.* Turner, 59–62.
247. *It would not be easy.* Turner, 78. (Source not cited).
248. *The human soul.* Aquinas, *Summa Theologica*, Ques. 75, Part I.
249. *One should also consider.* Thomas Aquinas, *Commentary on the First Epistle to the Corinthians*, No. 986, Fabian Archer, O.P., trans., http://dhspriory.org/thomas/ SS1Cor.htm.
250. *In the resurrected state.* Aquinas, *Commentary*, No. 987.

251. *Some have interpreted.* Aquinas, *Commentary*, No. 984.
252. *For Aquinas.* Turner, 78.
253. *What we must not think.* Aquinas, *Commentary*, No. 999.
254. *But rather flesh.* Aquinas, *Commentary*, No. 1,000.
255. *After the resurrection.* Aquinas, *Commentaries on 1 Corinthians 15*, para. 1000.
256. *As to the personal.* Aquinas, *Summa Theologica* I, Ques. 77, Art. 8.
257. *For the soul.* Aquinas, *Summa Theologica* IIIa, Supp. 79, 2.
258. *Regarding the origins.* Aquinas, *Summa Theologica* I, Ques. 76, Art. 3; Ques. 118, Art. 2.
259. *This explains why.* Vernon Bourke, "St. Thomas Aquinas," *Encyclopedia of Philosophy*, ed. Paul Edwards (New York: Macmillan & The Free Press, 1972), 109. In contrast to current Catholic doctrine, Aquinas took the position that ensoulment occurs in stages, and the abortion of a fetus prior to quickening was not homicide. Aquinas, *Summa Theologica* I-II, Ques. 64, Art. 8; *Summa contra Gentiles*, II, 89.
260. *Aquinas also rejected.* Aquinas, *Summa Theologica* I, Ques. 90, Art. 1–2.
261. *During his lifetime.* Turner, 92–93.
262. *For the Averroist.* Turner, 94–95.
263. *I can write no more.* Chesterton, 64.
264. *He died.* McInerny and O'Callaghan, 2.
265. *Aquinas was canonized.* McInerny and O'Callaghan, 3.

CHAPTER FIVE

ESOTERIC CHRISTIANITY & THE FOURTH WAY

266. *Every real religion.* Ouspensky, *Search*, 304.
267. *Gurdjieff speaks.* Patterson, "Gurdjieff & Christianity," in *Gurdjieff: The Man, The Teaching, His Mission*, 520. As Patterson points out, Gurdjieff would disagree with the fundamental teaching of *exoteric* Christianity that Jesus is the only Son of God. Patterson notes, however, "it is only Jesus and Buddha that Gurdjieff speaks of as being 'Divine.'" Patterson, 520.
268. *All the great.* Gurdjieff, *All and Everything*, 1001. Gurdjieff notes that the difference among the religions is in the observance of

what are called rituals, which are adopted to suit the degree of the mental perfection of people of the given period. Gurdjieff, 1002.
269. *Reached the beings.* Gurdjieff, *All and Everything,* 734–35.
270. *Thoroughly distorted.* Gurdjieff, *All and Everything,* 703.
271. *During the Middle Ages.* Gurdjieff, *All and Everything,* 703.
272. *Had not only.* Gurdjieff, *All and Everything,* 703–04. Gurdjieff commented that a small group still in existence, known as the Brotherhood of the Essenes, has preserved the teachings of Jesus unchanged.
273. *To come from the Gospel.* Ouspensky, *Search,* 129.
274. *If the followers.* Gurdjieff, *All and Everything,* 1001.
275. *A religion that consists.* Ouspensky, *Search,* 73.
276. *Of faith, love, adoration.* Ouspensky, *Search,* 73.
277. *Intellectual, theoretical religion.* Ouspensky, *Search,* 73–74.
278. *Religions number one.* Ouspensky, *Search,* 73–74.
279. *There exists a Christianity.* Ouspensky, *Search,* 74.
280. *Gurdjieff tells us.* Ouspensky, *Search,* 44.
281. *All esoteric religious.* Ouspensky, *Search,* 44.
282. *This is esoteric.* Ouspensky, *Search,* 102.
283. *It will seem strange.* Ouspensky, *Search,* 302
284. *Was not invented.* Ouspensky, *Search,* 302.
285. *In an essay.* Patterson, *Spiritual Survival,* 277–78.
286. *For what is now called.* Augustine, *Retractations,* I, xiii, 3, in *Augustine: Earlier Writings,* trans. John H. S. Burleigh (Philadelphia: Westminster Press, 1953), 218–19.
287. *Some of these groups.* Bart D. Ehrman, "Christianity Turned on Its Head: The Alternative Vision of the Gospel of Judas," in *The Gospel of Judas,* Rodolphe Kasser, Marvin Meyer, and Gregor Wurst, eds. (Washington, DC: National Geographic Society, 2006), 84.
288. *Prior to the discovery.* Ehrman, "Christianity Turned on Its Head," 118. As Ehrman points out, once this group "sealed its victory over all of its opponents, it rewrote the history of the engagement—claiming that it had always been the majority opinion of Christianity, that its views had always been the views of the apostolic churches and of the apostles . . ." Ehrman, 118.
289. *These included gospels.* Ehrman, "Christianity Turned on Its Head," 117. Many modern biblical scholars believe that Mary Magdalene

was an apostle of Jesus, if not his wife or consort. *See e.g.*, Segal, *Life After Death*, 555–58.
290. *The orthodox relied.* Pagels, *Gnostic Gospels*, 14.
291. *For gnostics.* Marvin Meyer, "Introduction," *The Gospel of Judas*, Rodolphe Kasser, Marvin Meyer, and Gregor Wurst, eds. (Washington, DC: National Geographic Society, 2006), 7.
292. *The Gnostics proclaimed.* Roelof Van den Broek, "Gnosticism I: Gnostic Religion," *Dictionary of Gnosis and Western Esotericism* (Boston, MA: Brill Academic Publishers, 2006), 404.
293. *This gnosis provided.* Lance S. Owens, MD, *An Introduction to Gnosticism and the Nag Hammadi Library*, the Gnostic Society Library, http://gnosis.org/naghamm/nhlintro.html.
294. *Fundamental to all.* Pagels, *Gnostic Gospels*, 14–15.
295. *These are the secret.* Marvin Meyer, trans., "The Gospel of Thomas," in *The Secret Teaching of Jesus: Four Gnostic Gospels* (New York: Random House, 1986), 19.
296. *Genuinely puzzling.* Segal, 470.
297. *Zen koans.* Pagels, *The Gnostic Gospels*, xv.
298. *Since you asked me.* Marvin Meyer, trans., "The Secret Book of James," in *The Secret Teachings of Jesus: Four Gnostic Gospels* (New York: Random House, 1986), 3.
299. *The secret account.* Kasser, *The Gospel of Judas*, 19.
300. *Conviction that direct.* Stephan A. Hoeller, *The Gnostic Jung* (Wheaton, IL, 1982), 11, http://www.gnosis.org/naghamm/nhlintro.html
301. *The Gnostics also shared.* Owens, *An Introduction to Gnosticism*.
302. *Who we were.* Van den Broek, 405.
303. *For gnostics.* Ehrman, "Christianity Turned on Its Head," 84.
304. *For he who has not.* Van den Broek, 410, *citing*, *Book of Thomas the Contender*, NHC II, 138, 16–18.
305. *Rather the Kingdom.* Elaine Pagels, *Beyond Belief: The Secret Gospel of Thomas* (New York: Random House, 2013), 54, *citing*, *Gospel of Thomas*, 118, 6. Pagels has noted that in the *Gospel of Thomas*, Jesus ridiculed those who thought of the "Kingdom of God" in literal terms, as if it were a specific place. Pagels, *Gnostic Gospels*, 118.
306. *If you bring forth.* Meyer, "The Gospel of Thomas," 32.
307. *Before everything else.* Pagels, *Gnostic Gospels*, 127.

308. *When man comes to know.* Van den Broek, 415, *citing, Testimony of Truth*, NHC IX, 44, 30–45, 6.
309. *Jesus said.* Meyer, "The Gospel of Thomas," 19.
310. *Blessed is one.* Meyer, "The Gospel of Thomas," 24.
311. *When you make the two.* Meyer, "The Gospel of Thomas," 24.
312. *Knock upon yourself.* Pagels, *Gnostic Gospels*, 127, *citing, Teachings of Silvanus*, 85.24–106.14, NHL 356–361.
313. *These words which.* Ouspensky, *Search*, 104.
314. *Without self-knowledge.* Ouspensky, *Search*, 104. Patterson says that human beings are "bioplasmic machines." He notes that "The Fourth Way begins by accepting that man is a machine. He can only cease to be a machine by awakening to his mechanicality. The practices of the teaching bring him to this realization and are the preparation for his self-transformation and transcendence." Patterson, *Spiritual Survival*, 26.
315. *We live and act.* Ouspensky, *Search*, 121.
316. *To awake, to die.* Ouspensky, *Search*, 217.
317. *There is nothing new.* Ouspensky, *Search*, 144.
318. *Asleep, drunk, ignorant.* Meyer, *Secret Teachings of Jesus*, xvi.
319. *End the sleep.* Pagels, *Gnostic Gospels*, 127, *citing, Teachings of Silvanus*, 88.24–92.12, NHL 349–350.
320. *Enlightened those who were.* Van den Broek, 410, *citing, The Gospel of Truth*, NHCI, 118, 16–20.
321. *I found them all.* Meyer, "The Gospel of Thomas," 25.
322. *Therefore become seekers.* Francis E. Williams, trans., *The Apocrophon of James*, The Gnostic Society Library, http://gnosis.org/naghamm/jam.html.
323. *All religions speak.* Gurdjieff, *Views from the Real World*, 86.
324. *Is going nowhere.* Ouspensky, *Search*, 159.
325. *From a thousand petty.* Ouspensky, *Search*, 218.
326. *According to an ancient teaching.* Ouspensky, *Search*, 40.
327. *Gurdjieff explains that.* Ouspensky, *Search*, 41.
328. *Gurdjieff tells us.* Ouspensky, *Search*, 41. The causal body is further defined as the body "which bears the *causes* of its actions within itself, is independent of external causes, and is the *body of will*." *Search*, 41, fn. 1.
329. *Man lives in one room.* Ouspensky, *Search*, 44.
330. *Almost all these teachings.* Ouspensky, *Search*, 41.

331. *And all esoteric religious.* Ouspensky, *Search*, 40. Immortality, Gurdjieff tells us, is a quality we ascribe to people without a sufficient understanding of its meaning. Other qualities we ascribe but do not understand include "individuality, in the sense of an inner unity, a 'permanent and unchangeable I,' 'consciousness' and 'will.'" *Search*, 40.
332. *Only the man who possesses.* Ouspensky, *Search*, 44.
333. *Direct access to Paul's.* Elaine Pagels, *The Gnostic Paul: Gnostic Exegesis of the Pauline Letters* (Philadelphia, PA: Fortress Press, 1975), 1.
334. *While orthodox Christian theologians.* Pagels, *Gnostic Paul*, 1–2. According to Irenaeus, Tertullian, and other church fathers, Paul saw the Gnostics as "ministers of Satan" and utterly rejected the secret wisdom they taught. Pagels, 1.
335. *Valentinus, whose enemies.* Pagels, *Gnostic Gospels*, 94–95.
336. *According to Valentinus.* David Brons, *A Brief Summary of Valentinian Theology*, the Gnostic Society Library, citing (Luke 8:9–10 cf. Ireneus Against Heresies 1:3:1). http://gnosis.org/library/valentinus/Brief_Summary_Theology.htm.
337. *Paul's 'mysticism' has been.* Pagels, *Gnostic Paul*, 2, *quoting*, H. Ch. Puech and G. Quispel, "Introduction," *Epistula ad Rheginum (De Ressurrectione)*, Coptic text ed. and trans. M. Maline, H. Ch. Puech, G. Quispel (Zurich: Raschner, 1963), xiii, xxxi.
338. *Their anthropology, their Christology.* Pagels, *Gnostic Paul*, 10.
339. *Only those who have received.* Pagels, *Gnostic Paul*, 6.
340. *Thus the Valentinians.* Pagels, *Gnostic Paul*, 4.
341. *The followers of Valentinus.* Pagels, *Gnostic Gospels*, 41.
342. *They distinguished between.* Pagels, *Gnostic Paul*, 5–6. In a different context, they also distinguished between the pneumatic, psychic, and hylic (material) natures in the individual human being. *See* Van den Broek, 411. The treatise *On the Origins of the World*, discovered in the Nag Hammadi, NHC II 122, 1–9, also distinguishes between three types of human beings, Pneumatics, Psychics, and Choics (earthly people). Van den Broek, 411.
343. *As Pagels explains.* Pagels, *Gnostic Paul*, 6; 120–21.
344. *Thus when Paul refers*, Pagels, *Gnostic Paul*, 126.
345. *The ordinary body subsumed.* Segal, 429–30.
346. *Becoming like him.* Segal, 419, *quoting*, Phil. 3:10.

347. *But our commonwealth.* Segal, 419, *quoting*, Phil. 3:20–21.
348. *If we had an English word.* Segal, 419.
349. *Lowly body to His glorious.* Segal, 419.
350. *The new structure refers.* Ouspensky, *Search*, 41.
351. *The fourth body.* Gurdjieff tells us "the consciousness of the fourth body has complete power over the 'mental,' the 'astral,' and the physical bodies." Ouspensky, *Search*, 92.
352. *Spiritual reformation.* Segal, 421.
353. *It all depends on.* Segal, 420.
354. *This new, spiritual.* Segal, 430.
355. *They [the pneumatics] warrant.* Segal, 438.
356. *It is sown.* 1 Cor. 15:41.
357. *Paul teaches that instead.* Segal, 431.
358. *Paul tells his followers.* Segal, 433.
359. *Developed a notion.* Segal, 439–40.
360. *Needless to say.* Patterson, "Gurdjieff & Christianity," 520. As Patterson notes in this essay, Gurdjieff's view of the resurrection of Jesus Christ differs radically from accepted doctrine. Gurdjieff holds that if a person dies and is buried, "this being will never exist again, nor furthermore will he ever speak or teach again."
361. *Segal notes with surprise.* Segal, 420.
362. *Baptism as dying.* Pagels, *Gnostic Paul*, 3.
363. *Segal does not draw.* Segal does document meticulously the deep connection between Paul and mystical Judaism. Segal, 412–16. Gurdjieff tells us, "In order to understand the interrelation of these teachings, it must always be remembered that the ways which lead to the cognition of unity approach are like the radii of a circle moving towards the center; the closer they come to the center, the closer they approach one another." Ouspensky, *Search*, 285.
364. *It is just this death.* Gurdjieff, *All and Everything*, 1232–33.
365. *Savior comes he shines.* Pagels, *Gnostic Paul*, 125, interpreting Paul's language in Ephesians 5:14, "Awake, o sleeper, and arise from the dead, and Christ shall give you light."
366. *Whoever has come to know.* Meyer, *Gospel of Thomas*, 34.
367. *If one does not understand.* Pagels, *Gnostic Gospels*, 126, *citing*, *Dialogue of the Savior*, 134.1-22, NHL 234.
368. *The soul needs to follow.* Meyer, trans., "The Secret Book of John," in *The Secret Teaching of Jesus: Four Gnostic Gospels* (New York:

Random House, Vintage Books 1986), 82–83. Likewise, in *The Secret Book of James*, Jesus describes a hierarchy of spirit, soul and human reason when he tells his disciples, "So be filled with spirit but lacking in human reason, for human reason is only human reason, and the soul, too, is only soul." Meyer, *Secret Book of James*, 5.

369. *The Gospel of Judas*. Meyer, "Introduction," *Gospel of Judas*, 4.
370. *As Pagels describes*. Elaine Pagels and Karen L. King, *Reading Judas: The Gospel of Judas and the Shaping of Christianity* (New York: Penguin Books, 2008), 3.
371. *Betrays Jesus in the Gospel*. Meyer, "Introduction," *Gospel of Judas*, 4.
372. *This devoted and favorite*. Gurdjieff, *All and Everything*, 739.
373. *Not only the most faithful*. Gurdjieff, *All and Everything*, 740–41.
374. *Gurdjieff refers*. Patterson, "Gurdjieff & Christianity," 520.
375. *I shall tell you the mysteries*. Kasser, et al., *Gospel of Judas*, 23.
376. *Performed the greatest service*. Ehrman, "Christianity Turned on Its Head," 101.
377. *You will exceed all*. Ehrman, "Christianity Turned on Its Head," 101; Kasser, et al., *Gospel of Judas*, 43.
378. *Even greater than assisting*. Gurdjieff, *All and Everything*, 740–41. See also, 726–29.
379. *This Judas, now a Saint*. Gurdjieff, *All and Everything*, 741.
380. *One is a "gift."* Kasser, et al., *Gospel of Judas*, 40.
381. *The soul on loan*. Kasser, et al., *Gospel of Judas*, 40, fn. 124.
382. *The souls of every human*. Kasser, et al., *Gospel of Judas*, 30.
383. *Everything living*. Ouspensky, 85.
384. *Thus in the Gospel*. See e.g., *The Gospel of Mary*.
385. *If a man*. Gurdjieff, *Views from the Real World*, 215.
386. *Therefore those who have not*. Teresa Adams, "Gurdjieff & Pythagoras—The Hyperborean Apollo, Part II," *The Gurdjieff Journal*, Vol. 18, No. 2, 10.
387. *Pagels notes that*. Pagels and King, 82, 90.
388. *Parallels Paul*. Segal, 471.
389. *The Fourth Way*. Patterson, *Gurdjieff: The Man, The Teaching, His Mission*, 522.
390. *The truth itself*. Augustine, *Reconsiderations*, I, xii, 3.
391. *New spiritualized*. Segal, 420.

392. *Madness consists.* Aldous Huxley, *After Many a Summer Dies the Swan* (Chicago: Ivan R. Dee, 1993) 309.

AFTERWORD

393. [393] *Cloud of fine matters.* Ouspensky, *The Fourth Way: A Record of Talks and Answers to Questions Based on the Teaching of G. I. Gurdjieff* (New York: Vintage Books, 1971), 180.
394. *The whole secret.* Ouspensky, *Search*, 101–102
395. *Becomes master of his life.* Ouspensky, *Search*, 101–102.
396. *To understand this.* Gurdjieff included this lecture in the final chapter of *All and Everything: Beelzebub's Tales to His Grandson.* To fully comprehend all that is contained in this passage, we recommend you read *All and Everything* as Gurdjieff instructs.
397. *Distributed into corresponding.* Gurdjieff, *All and Everything*, 1230.
398. *For the drops.* Gurdjieff, *All and Everything*, 1229.
399. *The first liberation.* Gurdjieff, *All and Everything*, 1232.
400. *Constant unquenchable impulse.* Gurdjieff, *All and Everything*, 1232.
401. *If there is a soul.* Gurdjieff, *All and Everything*, 1232.
402. *Even Jesus Christ.* Gurdjieff, *All and Everything*, 1232–33.
403. *I leave my.* Maugham, *The Razor's Edge*, 1.

APPENDIX

Zoroastrianism

404. [404] *All those who will.* Jal Dastur Cursetji Pavry, *The Zoroastrian Doctrine of a Future Life from Death to Individual Judgment* (New York: AMS Press, 1965), 1.
405. *Gradually however.* Piloo Nanavutty, trans., *The Gathas of Zarathustra: Hymns in Praise of Wisdom* (Ahmedabad, India: Mapin Publishing, 1999), 12.
406. *An Arabian invasion.* Nanavutty, *The Gathas of Zarathustra*, 13. Additionally, with this invasion, Arabic gradually replaced the Persian language, Avestan, further obscuring the opportunities to understand the Zoroastrian sacred scriptures.

407. *As long as I.* Nanavutty, *The Gathas of Zarathustra*, 73.
408. *In the Avesta.* The *Gathas* are contained within the *Avesta*.
409. *I declare to you.* Nanavutty, *The Gathas of Zarathustra*, 124. (From the *Ushtavad Gatha*, Yasna 45:5)
410. *These faculties include.* Nanavutty, *The Gathas of Zarathustra*, 36–37.
411. *Zarathustra does not answer.* Laina Farhaat-Holzman, *Strange Birds from Zoroaster's Nest* (Oneanta, NY: Oneanta Philosophy Studies, 2000), 200.
412. *And as Ahura Mazda.* Edmond Bordeaux Szekely, *The Zend Avesta of Zarathustra* (Nelson, BC, Canada: International Biogenic Society, 1990), 7–8.
413. *We can better.* Patterson, *Georgi Ivanovitch Gurdjieff*, 563–64.
414. *Instead of being pawns.* Maneckji Nusservanji Dhalla, *History of Zoroastrianism* (New York: Oxford University Press, 1938), 73. By eliminating the need to propitiate the gods, Zarathustra's teaching sought to end animal sacrifice.
415. *The soul feels.* Mary Boyce, *Textual Sources for the Study of Zoroastrianism* (Chicago: University of Chicago Press, 1990), 80–81.
416. *The conscience of the wicked.* Nanavutty, *The Gathas of Zarathustra*, 151.
417. *So understand, O mortal men.* Nanavutty, *The Gathas of Zarathustra*, 80.

John Milton

418. [418] *In his book.* The Christadelphians are a modern religious sect who do not believe in the immortality of the soul but embrace the hope of resurrection to eternal life at the return of Christ. http://www.christadelphia.org/belief.php.
419. *When a man's.* C. S. Nott, *Journey Through This World* (London: Routledge & Kegan Paul, 1969), 54.
420. *According to Gurdjieff.* Nott, 55.
421. *John Milton's epic poem.* Saurat says of *Paradise Lost*: "The greatness of *Paradise Lost*, like the *Divine Comedy*, lies in the fact that both authors were not mere literary men, but men who had fought and suffered in the greatest enterprises of their time . . . and put into

their poetry the result of their experience of life and struggle. That is why *Paradise Lost*, like the *Divine Comedy*, is a universal and human poem and not merely a work of rhetoric." Denis Saurat, *Milton: Man and Thinker* (New York: Dial Press, 1925), 28.

422. *It was Milton's*. A. W. Verity, *Milton's Samson Agonistes* (London: Cambridge University, 1925), x.
423. *Although he was imprisoned*. Barbara K. Lewalski, *The Life of John Milton* (Malden, MA: Blackwell, 2003), 398.
424. *Several of his closest friends*. Lewalski, 398.
425. *In addition, Milton*. While the prevailing view is that Milton completed *De Doctrina* late in life, the actual date is not known. For example, James Holly Hanford, in his 1920 article "The Date of Milton's de Doctrina Christiana," acknowledges the prevailing opinion, but argues it was more likely completed much earlier, by 1660. James Holly Hanford, "The Date of Milton's de Doctrina Christiana," *Studies in Philology*, Vol. 17, No. 3, July 1920, 309–10 & 317–18.
426. *Milton's beliefs*. Bryan W. Ball, *The Soul Sleepers: Christian Mortalism from Wycliff to Priestly* (London: James Clarke, 2008), 97.
427. *Milton saw the Church's teaching*. John Milton, *A Treatise on Christian Doctrine*, Charles R. Sumner, trans. (London: Cambridge University, 1825), 189–90. Saurat refers to this text as *De Doctrina* throughout *Milton: Man and Thinker*.
428. *That the spirit of man*. Milton, *De Doctrina*, 190.
429. *Man is a living being*. Milton, *De Doctrina*, 190.
430. *Body and soul*. Saurat, 141.
431. *Soul and body are one*. Saurat, 146.
432. *For what could be more*. Milton, *De Doctrina*, 280.
433. *The death of the body*. Milton, *De Doctrina*, 278–79.
434. *Therefore, that bodily death*. Milton, *De Doctrina*, 279.
435. *God is the primary*. Milton, *De Doctrina*, 238.
436. *All things are*. Milton, *De Doctrina*, 180.
437. *The original matter*. Saurat, 302.
438. *This is the fundamental*. Saurat, 46.
439. *Cannot finally*. *De Doctrina*, 242.
440. *God is neither willing*. *De Doctrina*, 242.
441. *The covenant*. *De Doctrina*, 511.
442. *Naturally and normally*. Saurat, 143.

443. *A key element.* Saurat, 198.
444. *Were there no resurrection.* Milton, *De Doctrina*, 511.
445. *There are only two.* Milton, *De Doctrina*, 282.
446. *There is not even.* Milton, *De Doctrina*, 281.
447. *The same time when.* Milton, *De Doctrina*, 282.
448. *No recompense. De Doctrina*, 293.
449. *Every man will. De Doctrina*, 511.
450. *Called out. De Doctrina*, 285.
451. *On earth. De Doctrina*, 515.
452. *Christ with the Saints.* Milton, *De Doctrina*, 512.
453. *Rule of judgment.* Milton, *De Doctrina*, 514.
454. *By punishment.* Milton, *De Doctrina*, 517.
455. *For the damned.* Milton, *De Doctrina*, 520.
456. *The loss of the chief.* Milton, *De Doctrina*, 519.
457. *For the righteous.* Milton, *De Doctrina*, 521.
458. *The history of mankind.* Saurat, 196.
459. *We come closest.* Saurat, 310.
460. *The sect had its roots.* Wycliffe argued that Christians should rely only on the Bible as religious authority and not on the teachings of popes and clerics; he also professed a belief in predestination and of an "invisible church of the elect" made up of those predestined to be saved.
461. *A century later.* Tyndale translated the Bible into English directly from the Greek and Hebrew texts. Tyndale's Bible played a key role in the Protestant Reformation, not only in England but throughout Europe.
462. *Systematic exposition.* Ball, 97.
463. *In 1644.* Richard Overton, *Man's Mortality* (London: Overton, 1644), no page numbers.
464. *We meet with.* Saurat, 312.
465. *Mans mortallitie.* Overton, *Man's Mortality,* title page.
466. *The pamphlet.* Richard Overton, *Man Wholly Mortal* (London: 1655). *Man Wholly Mortal* was reissued in 1675. All citations are from the 1675 edition. http://name.umdl.umich.edu/A53583.0001.001
467. *The Hell-hatch'd.* Ball, 100. This was a term given by a Mortalist supporter of Overton.
468. *Distortion of the truth.* Ball, 100.

469. *After death.* Overton, *Man's Mortality*, 6–7.
470. *Man not his flesh.* Overton, *Man's Mortality*, 4.
471. *The ridiculous invention.* Overton, *Man's Mortality*, 9.
472. *Nothing remains.*Overton, *Man's Mortality*, 13.
473. *None ever entered.* Overton, *Man's Mortality*, 6.
474. *Nay Paul himself.* Milton, *De Doctrina*, 282. Saurat notes other similarities, such as Overton pointing out humorously the error of those who say that the body alone dies in consequence of sin, arguing that punishing the body with death when it is merely the soul's instrument for action would be the same "as if a Magistrate should hang the Hatchet, and spare the Man that beate a mans braines out with it." *Man's Mortality*, 4–5.
475. *Both come to the conclusion.* Saurat, 318.
476. *Instead Overton reiterates.* Saurat, 318.
477. *Milton knew.* Saurat, 319–20.
478. *That which is finite.* Overton, *Man Wholly Mortal*, 20.
479. *Likewise, the 1655 version.* Overton, *Man Wholly Mortal*, 23–24.
480. *And so there is.* Overton, *Man Wholly Mortal*, 24.
481. *The salvation.* Overton, *Man Wholly Mortal*, 53.
482. *This is an argument.* Milton, *De Doctrina*, 256–60.
483. *In Man Wholly.* Saurat, 321.
484. *Lifted their whole.* Saurat, 321.
485. *On account of.* Ball, 97. In modern times, a sect of approximately 50,000 members called the Christadelphians continue to hold the beliefs of the Mortalists.
486. *He tells us.* These were published under the title, *La pensee de Milton.* Saurat, v.
487. *The upper strata.* Saurat, v.
488. *As a result.* Part four also includes the chapters "Robert Fludd (1574–1637)" (Fludd was a contemporary of Milton's who was an expert on the Kabbalah) and "The Mortalists (1643–1655)."
489. *Milton evidently took.* Saurat, 282–83.
490. *The most striking.* Saurat, 282.
491. *That one reservation.* Saurat, 282, fn. 2.
492. *There is only one.* Saurat, 283.
493. *Sleeps as it were.* Nott, 54.
494. *But . . . in the state of death.* Nott, 54.

495. *It is entirely different.* In *In Search of the Miraculous*, Ouspensky notes that although Gurdjieff did not introduce the idea of recurrence into his exposition of the system, he referred several times to the idea of recurrence, chiefly in speaking of the lost possibilities of people who had approached the system and then had drawn away from it. P. D. Ouspensky, *Search*, 251. However, in response to a direct question, Gurdjieff told Ouspensky, "This idea of repetition . . . is not the full and absolute truth, but it is the nearest possible approximation of the truth. In this case truth cannot be expressed in words. But what you say is very near to it." *Search*, 250.

496. *While Milton may.* In his introduction to *De Doctrina*, Milton explains that both the text and his faith are based on scrupulous study of scripture: "Having taken the grounds of my faith from divine revelation alone, and on the other, having neglected nothing which depended on my own industry, I thought fit to scrutinize and ascertain for myself the several points of my religious belief, by the most careful perusal and meditation of the Holy Scriptures themselves." John Milton, *De Doctrina Christiana*, or *Treatise on Christian Doctrine*, Trans. Charles R. Sumner, [from the original Latin] (Cambridge University, 1825), 3. For Milton, divine revelation comes "from the Holy Scriptures alone, under the guidance of the Holy Spirit." *De Doctrina*, 10. While Saurat expounds on Milton's familiarity with Jewish esotericism through the *Kabbalah* and the *Zohar*, the ideas Saurat explores in chapter four, "Religion," which are also here explored, are largely unrelated to Jewish esotericism and are instead steeped in Christianity.

497. *Peculiar to Milton.* Saurat, *Milton: Man and Thinker*, 171.

498. *Esoteric Christianity. Search*, 102.

499. *It is this second.* Saurat, 171.

500. *Christ is the elect.* Saurat, 172.

501. *Men hereafter may discern.* John Milton, *Paradise Regained*, 1671 (DjVu Editions E-books, 2001) Book I, lines 164–67.

502. *This is a change.* John, iii, 13, quoted in *De Doctrina*, 298. "And the Word was made flesh, and dwelt among us, (and we beheld his glory, the glory as of the only begotten of the Father,) full of grace and truth." Milton, *De Doctrina*, 343.

503. *That is, the inward man.* Milton, *De Doctrina*, 342.

504. *Milton sometimes uses.* Milton, *De Doctrina*, 342 & 273.
505. *Employing Christian terminology. Search*, 41.
506. *There is one single I. Search*, 42.
507. *God after His own image.* Milton, *De Doctrina*, 342.
508. *New and supernatural.* Milton, *De Doctrina*, 342.
509. *Milton thus depicts.* Milton, *De Doctrina*, 342.
510. *It is obvious therefore.* Milton, *De Doctrina*, 324.
511. *Despite this pronouncement.* Milton, *De Doctrina*, 325.
512. *This calling is either.* Milton, *De Doctrina*, 334.
513. *God's special calling.* Milton, *De Doctrina*, 335.
514. *The natural mind and will.* Milton, *De Doctrina*, 336–37.
515. *We must also be.* Milton, *De Doctrina*, 341.
516. *Continue to the end.* Milton, *De Doctrina*, 394.
517. *Regarding these efforts. Search*, 32.
518. *This power of volition.* Milton, *De Doctrina*, 338.
519. *Milton does not believe.* Saurat, 174. This may be seen as relating to the higher being-bodies, which Gurdjieff says are "composed of substances which gradually become finer and finer, [and] mutually interpenetrate one another." *Search*, 40.
520. *And through Christ.* Milton, *De Doctrina*, 309.
521. *So in Paradise Regained.* Saurat, 177.
522. *And the will.* Saurat, 177–78.
523. *That is to be saved.* Saurat, 178.
524. *Milton's temptations.* From Matthew 4:1–11: "After fasting for forty days and forty nights, He was hungry. The tempter came to Him and said, 'If you are the Son of God, tell these stones to become bread.' Jesus answered, 'It is written: "Man shall not live on bread alone, but on every word that comes from the mouth of God.' Then the devil took Him to the holy city and had Him stand on the highest point of the temple. 'If you are the Son of God,' he said, 'throw yourself down. For it is written: "He will commend His angels concerning you and they shall lift you up in their hands, So that you will not strike your foot against a stone."' Jesus answered him, 'It is also written: "Do not put the Lord your God to the test."' Again, the devil took Him to a very high mountain and showed him all the kingdoms of the world and their splendor. 'All this I will give you,' he said, 'if you will bow down and worship me.' Jesus said to him, 'Away from me, Satan! For it is

written, "Worship the Lord your God and serve him only.'" Then the devil left him, and angels came and attended him."

525. *Turn stones into bread.* The Three Temptations are told in Matthew and Luke; the order of the temptations differs in these two Gospels. In Luke the temptation to leap from the temple is third, while in Matthew, it is second. Compare Matthew 4:1–11 with Luke 4:1–13.

526. *Which he, who comes.* Milton, *Paradise Lost* (1667), Book X, lines 1284–288.

527. *Man lives not by Bread.* Milton, *Paradise Regained*, Book I, lines 349–50.

528. *Here is where Milton.* Professor John Rogers, Engl-220, *Milton*, Lecture 22-*Paradise Regained*, Books III–IV (November 28, 2007), http://oyc.yale.edu/english/engl-220/lecture-22.

529. *Yet he who reigns.* Milton, *Paradise Regained*, Book II, lines 466–77.

530. *It is the greatest mistake.* Search, 53.

531. *Each I does what he likes.* Search, 53–54.

532. *Without this, nothing.* Search, 103.

533. *For to be a Christian.* Search, 74.

534. *The most telling.* Many critics of *Paradise Regained* compare the quality of the writing unfavorably to that of the earlier epic *Paradise Lost* lamenting the loss of the eloquence of *Paradise Lost*, some suggesting the aging Milton was spent. Perhaps there's another explanation—he is demonstrating what he now values and does not want the style of writing to interfere with the substance.

535. *Look once more e're.* Milton, *Paradise Regained*, Book IV, lines 236–41.

536. *To hear and learn.* Milton, *Paradise Regained*, Book IV, lines 254–55.

537. *Satan literally offers.* Milton, *Paradise Regained*, Book IV, line 281. Apparently Milton acquired a great library at his home. He may be poking fun at himself here. Rogers, Lecture 22.

538. *These rules will.* Milton, *Paradise Regained*, Book IV, lines 284–85.

539. *Think not but.* Milton, *Paradise Regained*, Book IV, lines 286–92.

540. *The first and wisest.* Milton, *Paradise Regained*, Book IV, lines 293–94.

541. *The aim of the Fourth Way.* All and Everything, 88, 145.

542. *Gurdjieff says it.* Search, 245–46.

543. *There on your planet. All and Everything*, 323.
544. *Truly learned beings. All and Everything*, 322.
545. *Storm disturbs Jesus' sleep. Paradise Regained*, Book IV, lines 407–26.
546. *As prince of an indifferent.* Northrop Frye, *The Typology of Paradise Regained, Modern Philology*, Vol. 53, No. 4, May 1956, University of Chicago, 236.
547. *[I want to] learn.* Milton, *Paradise Regained*, Book IV, lines 515–19.
548. *Cast thyself down.* Milton, *Paradise Regained*, Book IV, lines 555–59.
549. *Also it is written.* Milton, *Paradise Regained*, Book IV, lines 560–61.
550. *For Milton what man.* Frye, 237.

SELECTED BIBLIOGRAPHY

Adams, Teresa. "Gurdjieff and Pythagoras—The Hyperborean Apollo" Pt. 2, *The Gurdjieff Journal*, Arete Communications, Volume 18, Issue 2.

Anderson, Margaret. *The Unknowable Gurdjieff.* London: Arkana, 1991.

Aquinas. *Summa Theologica*. Fathers of the English Dominican Province, translated by New York: Benziger Bros., 1947.

Augustine. *City of God*. Translated by Gerald Walsh, et al. Garden City, NY: Doubleday/Image Books, 1958.

———. *Confessions*. Translated by Henry Chadwick. New York: Oxford University Press, 1998.

———. *On the Soul and Origins* I.10, translated in *Nicene and Post-Nicene Fathers*, series I, vol. V. http://www.ccel.org/fathers2/NPNF1-05-31.html.

———. *Augustine: Earlier Writings*. Translated by John H. S. Burleigh. Philadelphia: Westminster Press, 1953.

———. *The Fathers of the Church: Augustine, The Retractations*. Translated by Mary Bogen. Washington, DC: Catholic University Press, 1999.

Ball, Bryan W. *The Soul Sleepers: Christian Mortalism from Wycliff to Priestly.* London: James Clarke, 2008.

Bennett, J. G. *Making a New World.* Santa Fe, NM: Bennett Books, 1992.

Broderick, M., and A. A. Morton. *A Concise Dictionary of Egyptian Archaeology.* London: Metheun & Co., 1903.

Chesterson, G. K. *St. Thomas Aquinas.* New York: Sheed & Ward, 1933.

Dunn, James, and John Robertson. *Eerdman's Commentary on the Bible.* Grand Rapids, MI: Wm. B. Eerdman, 2003.

Emery, W. B. *Archaic Egypt.* London: Penguin, 1961.

Ehrman, Bart, and Andrew Jacobs, editors. *Christianity in Late Antiquity, 300–450 C.E.: A Reader.* New York: Oxford University Press, 2004.

Farhaat-Holzman, Laina. *Strange Birds from Zoroaster's Nest.* Oneanta, NY: Oneanta Philosophy Studies, 2000.

Foltz, Richard C. *Religions of the Silk Road.* New York: St. Martins Press, 1999.

Frankfort, Henri. *Kingship and the Gods: A Study of Ancient Near Eastern Religion as the Integration of Society and Nature.* Chicago: University of Chicago Press, 1978.

Gilson, Etienne. *The Spirit of Medieval Philosophy (Gifford Lectures 1933–35).* Notre Dame, IN: University of Notre Dame Press, 1991.

Gurdjieff, G. I. *All and Everything.* Aurora, OR: Two Rivers Press, 1993.

———. *Views from the Real World.* London: Arkana, 1972.

Kasser, Rodolphe, Marvin Meyer, and Gregor Wurst, editors. *The Gospel of Judas*. Washington, DC: National Geographic Society, 2006.

Kurzweil, Ray. *The Singularity Is Near*. New York: Viking, 2005.

Lamy, Lucie. *Egyptian Mysteries*. New York: Crossroad, 1981.

Laymon, Charles M., editor. *The Interpreter's One-Volume Commentary on the Bible*. Nashville, TN: Abingdon Press, 1991.

Lewalski, Barbara K. *The Life of John Milton*. Malden, MA: Blackwell, 2003.

Lieu, Samuel C. *Manichaeism in the Later Roman Empire and Medieval China: A Historical Survey*. Oxford, England: Manchester University Press, 1985.

Lockwood Foundation. *New American Standard Bible*. La Habra, CA: Foundation Press, 1997.

Maccoby, Hyam. *The Mythmaker: Paul and the Invention of Christianity*. New York: Harper & Row, 1986.

Markus, R. A. "St. Augustine," *Encyclopedia of Philosophy*. Edited by Paul Edwards. New York: Macmillan & the Free Press, 1972.

Maugham, W. Somerset. *The Razor's Edge*. New York: Doubleday, Doran, 1944.

McInerny, Ralph. *Aquinas*. Cambridge, UK: Polity Press & Blackwell Publishing, 2004.

Mendelson, Michael. "Saint Augustine." *Stanford Encyclopedia of Philosophy*. Edited by Edward N. Zalta. Winter 2012 ed.

Meyer, Marvin, translator. *The Secret Teachings of Jesus: Four Gnostic Gospels*. New York: Random House, Vintage Books, 1986.

Milton, John. *A Treatise on Christian Doctrine*. Translated by Charles R. Sumner. London: Cambridge University, 1825.

———. *Paradise Lost*. 1671. DjVu Editions E-Books, 2001.

———. *Paradise Regained*. 1671. DjVu Editions E-Books, 2001.

Nanavutty, Piloo, translator. *The Gathas of Zarathustra: Hymns in Praise of Wisdom*. Ahmedabad, India: Mapin Publishing, 1999.

Niederbacher, Bruno. "The Human Soul: Augustine's Case for Soul-Body Dualism." *The Cambridge Companion to Augustine*. Edited by David Merconi and Eleanor Stump. Cambridge, UK: Cambridge University Press, 2014.

Nott, C. S. *Journey Through This World*. London: Routledge & Kegan Paul, 1969.

Ouspensky, P. D. *In Search of the Miraculous*. New York: Harcourt, Brace and World, 1949.

Overton, Richard. *Man's Mortality*. London: Overton, 1644.

Owens, Lance S. *An Introduction to Gnosticism and the Nag Hammadi Library*. The Gnostic Society Library. http://gnosis.org/naghamm/nhlintro.html.

Pagels, Elaine. *Adam, Eve, and the Serpent*. New York: Vintage Books, 1989.

———. *Beyond Belief: The Secret Gospel of Thomas*. New York: Random House, 2013.

———. *The Gnostic Gospels*. New York: Vintage Books, 1979.

———. *The Gnostic Paul: Gnostic Exegesis of the Pauline Letters*. Philadelphia, PA: Fortress Press, 1975.

Pagels, Elaine and Karen L. King. *Reading Judas: The Gospel of Judas and the Shaping of Christianity.* New York: Penguin Books, 2008.

Paton, Lewis Bayles. *Spiritism and the Cult of the Dead in Antiquity.* New York: MacMillan, 1921.

Patterson, William Patrick. *Georgi Ivanovitch Gurdjieff: The Man, The Teaching, His Mission.* Fairfax, CA: Arete Communications, 2014.

———. *The Life and Significance of George Ivanovitch Gurdjieff, Part I: Gurdjieff in Egypt: The Origin of Esoteric Knowledge. Film.* Fairfax, CA: Arete Communications, 2000.

———. *Introduction to Gurdjieff's Fourth Way: From Selves to Individual Self to The Self.* Film. Fairfax, CA: Arete Communications, 2012.

———. *Ladies of the Rope: Gurdjieff's Special Left Bank Women's Group.* Fairfax, CA: Arete Communications, 1999.

———. *Spiritual Pilgrimage: Mr. Gurdjieff's Father's Grave.* Film. Fairfax, CA, Arete Communications, 2016.

———. *Spiritual Survival in a Radically Changing World-Time.* Fairfax, CA: Arete Communications, 2009.

———. *Voices in the Dark.* Fairfax, CA: Arete Communications, 2000.

Pavry, Jal Dastur Cursetji. *The Zoroastrian Doctrine of a Future Life from Death to Individual Judgment.* New York: AMS Press, 1965.

Platcher, William and Derek Nelson. *A History of Christian Theology: An Introduction.* Louisville, KY: Westminster John Knox Press, 2013.

Plato. *The Works of Plato.* Translated by B. Jowett. New York: Random House, 1956.

Reed, Bika. *Rebel in the Soul.* Rochester, VT: Inner Traditions, 1997.

Saurat, Denis. *Milton: Man and Thinker.* New York: Dial Press, 1925.

Schwaller de Lubicz, Isha. *Her-Bak: Egyptian Initiate.* New York: Inner Traditions, 1979.

———. *The Opening of the Way: A Practical Guide to the Wisdom of Ancient Egypt.* Rochester, VT: Inner Traditions, 1981.

Schwaller de Lubicz, R. A. *Nature Word.* West Stockbridge, MA: Lindisfarne Press, 1982.

———. *Sacred Science: The King of Pharaonic Theocracy.* Rochester, VT: Inner Traditions, 1988.

———. *The Temple in Man.* Brookline, MA: Autumn Press, 1977.

———. *The Temple of Man.* Rochester, VT: Inner Traditions, 1998.

———. *The Temples of Karnak.* Rochester, VT: Inner Traditions, 1999.

Segal, Alan F. *Life After Death: A History of the Afterlife in the Religions of the West.* New York: Doubleday, 2004.

Stanley, David M. *The Gospel of St. Matthew.* Collegeville, MN: The Liturgical Press, 1967.

Szekely, Edmond Bordeaux. *The Zend Avesta of Zarathustra.* Nelson, BC, Canada: International Biogenic Society, 1990.

Tabor, James D. *Paul and Jesus: How the Apostle Transformed Christianity.* New York: Simon & Schuster, 2012.

Turner, Denys. *Thomas Aquinas: A Portrait.* New Haven, CT: Yale University Press, 2013.

Van den Broek, Roelof. "Gnosticism I: Gnostic Religion." *Dictionary of Gnosis and Western Esotericism*. Boston, MA: Brill Academic Publishers, 2006.

Verity, A. W. *Milton's Samson Agonistes*. London: Cambridge University, 1925.

Ware, Timothy. *The Orthodox Church: New Edition*. London: Penguin Books, 2nd ed., 1997.

Whitehead, Alfred North. *Process and Reality*. New York: Simon & Schuster, the Free Press, 1979.

Zuckerman, Phil. *Living the Secular Life: New Answers to Old Questions*. New York: Penguin Books, 2014.

INDEX

A

Aeterni Patris (Pope Leo XIII), 64
Aquinas, Thomas
   Commentaries on 1 Corinthians 15, 69
   Commentaries on the Epistles of St. Paul, 67
   Commentary
      No. 999, *68*
      No. 1,000, *69*
   On Being and Essence, 64
   On the Eternity of the World, 64
   On There Being Only One Intellect, 64
   On the Principles of Nature, 64
   Summa Theologica, 64–65, 69
Archaic Egypt (Emery), 29
Aristotle, 53, 63–67, 69, 126, 143n236
Augustine, 41, 52–64, 68, 70, 74, 92, 110, 117, 140n178, 141n183, 142n221, 143n236
   City of God, 56, 58–60, 62
   Confessions, 56, 56n20, 57
   Letter 166, 62
   On the Immortality of the Soul, 56–57, 62
   On the Magnitude of the Soul, 56, 62
   On the Origins of the Soul, 56
   On the Two Souls, Against the Manichees, 56
   Reconsiderations, 56, 74
   Sermon 362, 56, 58
   Soliloquies, 57
Averroes, 69

B

Buddhism, xin1

C

Christ, Jesus, 30, 39–47, 50–52, 71–72, 74–79, 81, 84, 86, 88–91, 93, 98, 123–28
Christianity, xi, xvi, 2, 30, 33, 37–40, 45, 47–48, 54–55, 57–58, 71–75, 80, 83–84, 92–93, 98, 101, 120–21, 137n121, 140n178, 144n267, 145n288, 156
Catholic Church, xiv, 48, 52, 54
Corinthians, 51
Elizabeth, 43
garden of Gethsemane, 43, 81

John, Gospel of, 40–41, 43–45, 113
John the Baptist, 43
Last Supper, 44, 90, 90n31
Luke, Gospel of, 40–46
Magdalene, Mary, 76, 145n117
Mark, Gospel of, 40–45
Martha, 44
Matthew, Gospel of, 40–45
New Testament, 40–42, 45, 76
Paul. *See* Paul
pneumatology, 49
Sermon on the Mount, 44
Constantine, 55

E

Egypt, xvi, 24, 26, 26n14, 27, 29–30, 34, 36–38, 73–74, 89, 93, 98
Al-Kemi, 27
Amenhotep III, 28
Amon-Re, 28
Atum, 33
Ba, 34–36
Horus, 29–30
ia, 34
iaaw, 34
Isis, 30
Ka, 34–36
Ka-djet, 35
Maât, 36
Me, 35–36
neter, 26, 30–31, 33, 35–36
Osiris, 30
Ptah, 33–34
Set, 30, 136n92
Shemsu-Hor, 29

Temple of Edfu, 30–31
Temple of Man, 28, 133, 134n59, 134–36, 166
Emery, W. B., 29
esoteric Christianity, xvi, 2, 37–38, 48, 71–93, 120–21
Gnosticism, 75–76
Gospel of Judas, 76, 78, 78n27, 89–91
Gospel of Mary Magdalene, 76
Gospel of Peter, 76
Gospel of Phillip, 76
Gospel of Thomas, 76–77, 78n27, 79
Gospel of Truth, 81, 84–85, 147
and Gurdjieff, 71–76, 88–93
metaschematisei, 86–87
Paul and Gnosticism, 75, 78n27, 84–88, 90n31, 92–93
pneumatic, 50, 85–87, 92, 148n342
pneumatics, 85–87, 148n342
Secret Book of James, 76–77, 81
soma physikon, 49
soma pneumatikon, 50, 58, 84, 86–87, 92
soma psychikon, 92
soma sarkikon, 49
spiritual bodies, 82–83, 86–87
symmorphon, 86–87
Teachings of Silvanus, 81
Testimony of Truth, 79, 147

F

Fourth Way, The, xiv–xvi, 2, 2n5, 6–8, 22–24, 33, 37–38, 71–73, 73n25, 74–75, 84, 90n31, 92–93, 98, 110, 120, 125–26

Autoegocratic, 18
being-Impulsakri, 20
being-Partkdolg-duty, 13–15, 17, 20–21, 23
buffers, 13, 13n10
   centers, thinking, emotional, and moving/instinctive/sexual, 8, 21
conscience, xvi, 12–13, 23, 104
conscious, consciousness, xvi, 6–9, 12–14, 16, 19–23, 82–83, 92, 96–97
Djartklom, 20
Holy Sun Absolute, 18–20
"I"s, 4–5, 13, 21, 23
Kesdjan or astral body, 9, 11, 11n9, 12, 14–15, 15n11, 16, 21, 22n12, 23, 82–83, 133n34
   law of three (Triamazikamno), 17, 21, 33
Megalocosmos, 17–18, 20–22, 91
   mental body (third being-body), 9, 18, 82
Okidanokh, 20–21
physical body, xv, 8–9, 11, 14–17, 19, 21–22, 22n12, 23, 73n25, 82–83, 93, 96
Rascooarno, 16
Ray of Creation, 9n8, 18–19, 92
self-observation, 6–7, 21–23, 93
   self-remembering, 6–7, 20–23, 90n31, 93
self-sensing, 6, 20–23, 93
Theomertmalogos, 9, 16, 20
Trogoautoegocrat, 18, 20
Frederick II, 64

G

gnosis, 76–78, 84–85
Gnostic Gospels, 40, 75–76, 78–79, 81, 89, 92, 101
   Apocryphon of James, 76
   Book of Thomas the Contender, 79, 146
   Dialogue of the Savior, 89, 149
   Gospel of Judas, 76, 78, 78n27, 89–92
   Gospel of Peter, 76
   Gospel of Phillip, 76
   Gospel of Thomas, 76–77, 78n27, 79, 81, 88, 92, 146n305
   Nag Hammadi, 75–77, 78n27, 84, 148n342
   Testimony of Truth, 79
Gurdjieff, Georgi Ivanovitch, xv–1, 1n4, 2–7, 9, 9n8, 11, 11n9, 12, 14–15, 15n11, 16–18, 20–22, 24, 29, 33, 37–38, 41, 70–76, 80, 80n29, 81–83, 86, 88–93, 96–98, 102n34, 108, 110, 117–22, 125–26, 129, 133n34, 134n57, 144nn267-268, 145n272, 148n331, 149n351, 149n360, 149n363, 151n396
   All and Everything, 15n11, 18, 76, 89, 102n34, 108, 127, 133n34, 144n268, 145n272, 151n396
   See also Fourth Way, The

J

Judaism, xi, 72, 101, 149

K

Kabbalah, 118, 155–56
Knowles, David, 63

L

Leo XIII, 64

M

Manichaeism, 55–56, 140–41
Maugham, W. Somerset, xii, 97n32, 98
metaschematisei, 86–87
Milton, John
   De Doctrina Christiana, 110–13, 116–17, 153, 156
   Paradise Lost, 108, 110, 112, 120, 123, 152–53, 158
   Paradise Regained, 110, 120, 122–24, 127, 158
   Samson Agonistes, 109–10
Mortalists, 108, 110, 114–19, 155n485

N

Nott, C. S., 108, 110, 117–19
   Journey through This World, 108, 118

O

Ouspensky, P. D., 9n8, 15n11, 80, 119, 156n495
   In Search of the Miraculous, 9n8, 11n9, 13n10, 15n11, 19, 73n25, 80n29, 147n314, 148n331, 149n363, 156n495, 157n519

Overton, Richard, 115–17, 154–55
   Man's Mortality, 115–16, 155
   Man Wholly Mortal, 115–17

P

Pagels, Elaine, 54, 59, 59n21, 60, 75n26, 76–77, 85, 88–89, 92, 101n33, 140n178, 146n305, 148n334, 149n365
   Beyond Belief: The Secret Gospel of Thomas, 146n305
   The Gnostic Gospels, 75n26, 101n33
   The Gnostic Paul: Gnostic Exegesis of the Pauline Letters, 85, 148n342, 149n365
Papyrus of Turin, 26n14, 29, 135n79
parousia, 51
Patterson, William Patrick, 1n5, 6–7, 10, 30–31, 73n24, 74, 131n4, 144n267, 147n314, 149n360
Paul, 41, 44–55, 57–58, 63–64, 67–70, 75, 78, 84–88, 90n31, 90, 92–93, 113, 116, 139, 148–49
   Acts of the Apostles, 45–47, 139n147
   and church fathers, 45, 48
   and Gnosticism, 75, 84–85
   Corinthians, 46, 50–51, 64, 67–68, 70
   Galatians, 46, 51
   Philippians, 46, 86
   and Valentinus, 75, 84–85
Pentland, Lord John, 6
Plato, 1n5, 46, 49, 53–54, 54n18, 57, 62, 69, 110, 126
Plotinus, 56
Porphyry, 56
Ptah, 33–34

R

Razor's Edge, The (Maugham), xii, 97n32, 98

S

Saurat, Denis, 108, 111–12, 114–20, 122, 152–53, 155–56
Scholasticism, 65
Schwaller de Lubicz, Isha, 25n13, 34, 134n69
Schwaller de Lubicz, R. A., 24–26, 26n14, 27, 29–30, 134n59
Segal, Alan, 48–49, 55, 58, 77, 79n28, 84, 86–88, 90n31, 92–93, 140n168
Set, 30–31, 136n92
Shemsu-Hor, 26, 29
Silvanus, 79, 81, 147
  Teachings of Silvanus, 81
soma physikon, 49
soma pneumatikon, 50, 58, 84, 86–87, 92
soma psychikon, 49–50, 84, 86–87, 92, 140n168
soma sarkikon, 49
Strauss, Leo, 1n5
symmorphon, 87

T

Theudas, 84
Turner, Denys, 66–67, 67n22, 143n229
Tyndale, William, 114, 154

V

Valentinus, 75, 84–85
  The Gospel of Truth, 84–85
  Interpretation of the Gnosis, 84
  Tripartite Tractate, 84
  Valentinians, 84–86, 88

W

Ware, Timothy, 39n15, 84n30
  The Orthodox Church, New Edition, 39n15, 84n30
Wycliffe, John, 114, 154

Z

Zohar, 118–19, 156
Zoroastrianism, 75, 101–2, 104–5, 107, 151–52
  Ahura Mazda, 101, 103–5, 107, 152
  Angra Mainyu, 105–7
  Asha, 103, 105
  Avesta, 104, 151–52, 166
  Gathas, 102, 104–6, 151–52, 164
  Parsees, 102
  Zarathustra, 101–3, 105–7, 151–52, 164, 166